POSITIVE DISCIPLINE

Help Your Child Develop Self Discipline,
Responsibility and Build Comunication
From Toddler to Teenager

WRITTEN BY
Susan Garcia

CONTENTS

PART 1 10

Introduction 11

Chapter 1: Discipline vs. Punishment 19

Chapter 2: The Main Goals of Discipline 25

Chapter 3: How it Worked Before 32

Chapter 4: What is Positive Discipline 37

Chapter 5: Positive discipline and your child's development 40

   Positive Parenting and Emotional development in Kids 42

      0-13 months of emotional development 44

      13-36 months Toddlers emotional development 47

      Preschoolers (3-5 years) Emotional Development 50

      6-10 years of elementary schoolers emotional development 53

      Positive discipline and brain development . 60

Chapter 6: The basics of positive discipline 68

   Connect with your child 68

Set clear firm limits in a loving and respectful way 77

Good children and bad behavior 81

Give guidance and offer choices 83

Bribes vs. Praise and Encouragement 86

Teach empathy 94

Name emotions 96

Feelings word chart 98

Choose your battles 99

Chapter 7: Parenting styles and discipline 123

Authoritarian parent 124

Permissive parent 127

Neglectful parent 128

Authoritative parent 130

The exception 132

Conflicting parenting styles and their effect on discipline 133

How to harmonize parenting styles and discipline as a team 134

The bottom lines 137

Reading list 141

PART 2 142

Introduction 143

Chapter one ... 147

What is Positive Parenting? ... 147

A Teen's Brain and how it Changes ... 150

Hormonal Changes in Teens and how They Affect Them ... 157

Physical Changes and What They Mean to your Teen ... 161

Teens, Friends, and Parents ... 167

Chapter Two ... 176

How Parenting Styles Influence Your Teen ... 176

The Fight for Control: The Drill Sergeant ... 177

The Rescue Parent: Helicopter and Permissive Parent ... 182

The Consultant Parents: Positive Parenting ... 185

Do Children Raised by Consultant Parents Still Rebel? ... 192

Chapter Three ... 196

How to Raise Responsible Teens ... 196

A Teen's Self-Concept ... 198

Where do you go from here? ... 209

Building your Teen's Self-Concept ... 209

- Help teens feel good about themselves ... 209
- How to use Convert Messages ... 211

    Responsibility and Self-Concept 213

    Let Teens Own their Problems 214

Chapter Four 218

How to Connect with your Teen 218

  How to Listen to Teens and Finally get them to Listen 224

  Help your Teen Communicate their Feelings . 229

  The Fight for Control and How it can Foster Connection... 233

  How to use Mistakes as Opportunities to Connect and Learn... 238

Chapter Five 243

Enabling vs. Empowering 243

  How to Teach your Teens Life Skills 247

    Look for Teachable Moments 247

    Use your Teen's Interests to Teach 248

    Teach your Teens how to Plan.................... 249

    Encourage Routines.................................... 253

    Don't be Afraid to ask for Help................... 254

Chapter Six 256

What to do About Scary Behavior 256

  Friends or Lack Thereof 256

  What if you Hate your Teen's Friends? 257

    Drugs and Alcohol Abuse................................. 258

    Teen Sex, Pregnancy and Sexually Transmitted Diseases 262

    Suicidal Behavior 264

    Kids who Won't Move Out 265

Conclusion 268

References 270

© Copyright 2019 - All rights reserved.

The content contained within this book may not be reproduced, duplicated or transmitted without direct written permission from the author or the publisher.

Under no circumstances will any blame or legal responsibility be held against the publisher, or author, for any damages, reparation, or monetary loss due to the information contained within this book. Either directly or indirectly.

Legal Notice:

This book is copyright protected. This book is only for personal use. You cannot amend, distribute, sell, use, quote or paraphrase any part, or the content within this book, without the consent of the author or publisher.

Disclaimer Notice:

Please note the information contained within this document is for educational and entertainment purposes only. All effort has been executed to present accurate, up to date, and reliable, complete information. No warranties of any kind are declared or implied. Readers acknowledge that the author is not engaging in the rendering of legal, financial, medical or professional advice. The content within this book has been derived from various sources. Please consult a licensed professional before attempting any techniques outlined in this book.

By reading this document, the reader agrees that under no circumstances is the author responsible for any losses, direct or indirect, which are incurred as a result of the use of information contained within this document, including, but not limited to, — errors, omissions, or inaccuracies.

Download the Audio Book Version of This Book for FREE

If you love listening to audio books on-the-go, I have great news for you. You can download the audio book version of this book for FREE just by signing up for a FREE 30-day audible trial! See below for more details!

Audible Trial Benefits

As an audible customer, you will receive the below benefits with your 30-day free trial:

- FREE audible book copy of this book
- After the trial, you will get 1 credit each month to use on any audiobook
- Your credits automatically roll over to the next month if you don't use them
- Choose from Audible's 200,000 + titles
- Listen anywhere with the Audible app across multiple devices
- Make easy, no-hassle exchanges of any audiobook you don't love
- Keep your audiobooks forever, even if you cancel your membership
- And much more

Scan the code below to get started!

BONUS

Thank you for purchasing my book. I have a gift for you. A collection of printable worksheets for your little children for FREE.

Scan the code below

PART 1

Positive Discipline for Toddler

Introduction

Parents have for a long time tried to figure out the relationship between them and their kids. While there are many techniques that one can use to strengthen this relationship, positive parenting is the number one way to raise happy, disciplined children. Parents are the most concern with their kids' happiness, but they want to be happy as well.

We want to enjoy being parents and not have such a hard time correcting our kids' behavior. For us, it would be bliss if our kids would not throw tantrums, talk back, did their homework on time, went to bed on time, and collected their toys leaving the house, and their rooms clean at all times. However, this is hardly ever the case, even with older children who know what they ought to do.

We scold, we talk, we repeat, and we give up. Sometimes we decide that sanity is better than all the yelling and policing we are subjected to. "If a day would go by without me yelling, that would be like winning the lottery," we laugh with our friends over coffee.

However, maybe we have this all wrong. Maybe the yelling and talking and nagging are producing more problems than it is helping us raise healthy, disciplined and happy kids. Maybe we need to try another approach.

Imagine starting a kitchen garden to grow vegetables for your family. When you start with your seedlings, it will not look like much. You work your way out to watering, weeding and keeping insects, diseases, and birds away. After a few short weeks, your garden looks beautiful, and your family can enjoy it.

Similarly, raising children is like maintaining a garden. When your child first arrives, they are a blank canvass, like a seed, and how you take care of them by nurturing them through the difficult emotions of childhood determines how they will turn out as adults. Rearing children requires developing effective parenting skills, just like gardening.

Parents have agreed that there is no child-rearing manual, and while this is correct, research by psychologists and social scientists have revolutionized how children are raised by conducting experiments that help us understand children better. Research by Jean Piaget revealed that children do not understand situations in the same way adults do. Expecting children to act like 'mini adults' and behave will, therefore, get us nowhere.

Is all lost then? Are we stuck with kids who cannot listen and behave the way they should? Is parenting going to be an impossible uphill task? Lucky for us, the answer is no! Children are born ready to learn, and the first person they learn from is you and me. As a parent, modeling good and acceptable behavior is the first step in raising kids. We have heard people say that 'kids will do as you do, not as you say' and it is true. Imagine then what we are modeling when we scold them guns blazing and send them to their rooms amid abuse and threats! Is this how we would like them to behave? So why do we model it?

If we are honest, we have used how we were raised as a foundation for raising our kids. If we were punished, we are prone to punish as well. If our parents were kind and respectful, we are likely to be kind and respectful. While we may carry hurt feelings in us from our childhood, healing these past pain helps us become better parents than our parents. Without healing, we are likely to inflict the same pain in our kids, create the same resentment we feel, and undoubtedly continue the cycle. However, we have to adopt a different method, so this cycle ends with us. By rewriting our past, we can write the future.

Once our past pain is healed, we must rewire our brains to positive parenting. A mental diet is not an easy diet. Like joining the gym, you are going against your body's current and forcing it to start swimming uphill. Charles Duhigg has demonstrated this in his book "*The Power of Habit; Why We Do What We do in Life and Business*." A parent prone to use punishment uses it with so much ease because it has already become a habit, formed slowly from how they were raised to how they have been using it on other kids, their peers, and now their kids.

To break the cycle, and ultimately use positive parenting techniques, we must make a conscious decision to break the habit. Easier said than done, but it is possible. When your child misbehaves, the routine is to use some form of punishment (yell, time-out, threaten, spank). What we want to achieve is connecting with our child, understanding where they are coming from and using the misbehavior as a platform to correct bad behavior and teach a life skill such as anger management, empathy, responsibility, timekeeping, among others.

Emotions are the center of living. Helping your child understand their emotions is helping them live a happy and successful life. We do what we do because of how it makes us feel. Let us strive to teach our kids, every day, how to handle their emotions, and they will learn how to handle their behavior. Before we discipline, we must consciously ask ourselves why did my child react like that? What can I teach? How can I best teach this lesson?

A child does not wake up and decide to be naughty. They have a reason behind every behavior, and they have desires they want to express, just like you and me. By knowing where they are coming from, we understand the desire they wish to be met, and use this as a teaching platform to show kids how to meet their desire without misbehaving.

The journey is only tough when you start. Positive parenting is not something you might be used to and snapping every once in a while, is ok. Like our kids, we are learning a new skill, and every skill takes time to master. The more you exercise a muscle, the stronger it becomes, and a mental muscle is no different. The more we continue to follow positive parenting principles, the more it is engraved in our minds that this is the new default setting.

Positive parenting is not about immediate gratification and instant pleasure, for our kids or us. It's about setting it up right for kids, and ourselves, to enjoy long-term happiness in life.

Sometimes instant gratification is what we need, and it is achievable without using punishment. If you are in a public place and your child throws a tantrum, you want them to stop. This is a short-term goal for every discipline act. You also want to make sure that they do not repeat the behavior in question, which is a long-term goal for disciplining your child.

When we understand how our kids' brains are developing, we are better placed to understand that their behavior is either being controlled by their rational mind or their irrational mind. When the irrational mind, also called the reptilian brain, is engaged, your child will not cooperate no matter how much you try. Sure, threatening them and spanking them will get them to stop, but the little fellow is left confused and wonders if being himself is a crime that he must be punished for it. It is everyone's nature to use our reptilian brain, and naturally, we want to either fight or flee. However, that does not mean that we should.

Parents must learn to disengage their kid's irrational mind and engage their rational mind. When emotions are high, let them calm down. Connect with your child and comfort them. Allow them to feel their emotions and then teach them how to handle it better next time. Do not lecture them, instead engage them in a dialogue where you can both look for a suitable solution. You demonstrate patience, mastery of your own emotions, and problem-solving skills, all necessary for a happy child and an equally happy parent.

In every home setting, ideas are bound to clash. Parents are two people from different backgrounds with different beliefs coming together to raise this little human. When ideas clash, it is time to team up and draw a roadmap to guide you in the future. Remember we are not perfect, and we will make mistakes. However, undermining your partner in the presence of your child is confusing the child and losing your authority as a parent. A united front creates stability for the children.

Keeping it together is not always easy. A good parent can often snap and lose it. Everyone has a limit so if you can catch up with a friend, sleep early, take up cycling, jog, go for a swim, and have a spa treatment it will do you good. Live a little away from parenthood. These are great ways to maintain equilibrium. Joining a positive parenting support group would be better if you feel completely overwhelmed no matter what you do. Having someone to exchange ideas with and be honest about your feelings with is important. If you need a support group, reach out.

Knowing what to do and not doing it is the danger of learning. It is one thing to pick up a book such as this one and another thing to implement the principals outlined in the chapters to follow. Being a parent does not have to be so hard. It can be enjoyable if you take a step at a time towards raising children in a positive environment that is conducive for you and them. So, don't bite more than you can chew. Start with one thing at a time and keep adding to the list. Parenting is not a sprint; it is a marathon. If you keep training and using positive parenting methods, you will win the race and raise independent, centered children.

Chapter 1: Discipline vs. Punishment

Children are capable of thinking. The only difference between how their brains work and ours is the level of maturity and development. The guidance of a parent/guardian is a crucial role in helping children develop, especially where discipline is concerned.

Parents sometimes feel at a loss when it comes to getting their kids to act respectfully. Kids often argue, are disrespectful and will climb on the top of the table during dinner whenever they get a chance. As a parent, you often feel frustrated and find yourself uttering the same phrases over and over again. "Don't do that. Stop It! You are going to hurt yourself."

The constant battles witnessed during homework, bedtime and meal times is evidence of the struggle parents are engaged in continuously with their children. If you experience any of these frustrations, you are not alone.

Discipline is a fundamental aspect of raising children, but most parents often mistake it with punishment. Discipline comes from the word 'disciple,' which means, to teach, train, or to instruct. Thus, it is an act of teaching children how they should behave and respond to situations emotionally and intellectually.

Parents are encouraged to use positive discipline methods that involve listening, responding and connecting with a child as opposed to reacting to their bad behavior. However, this is not easy especially when a child is not cooperating in a situation where one is tired and stressed up; it is always easier to punish in such cases.

According to the dictionary, punishment is the infliction of retribution for a committed offense. In simple terms, to punish is to inflict suffering as a penalty for bad behavior purposely. That does not sound so appealing, not to you or your child.

Let's take an example; your six-year-old child is out in the yard playing with dirt. She just learned how to plant a seed and nurture a plant, and she is trying to grow cabbage from a random seed she collected yesterday on her way home from school. She rushes into the house all muddy and pulls you to see her plant.

As she was busy with her experiment, you were busy finishing the hours of kitchen cleaning you have been postponing for the last three weeks. Now, it's all muddy and so are your clothes, you immediately react by yelling at her over the mess she has made. "You won't play with mud again if you can't keep it outside" you threaten her as you march her to the bathroom for a scrub.

While this may not seem to be a problem, the damage your child will experience from this punishment is far greater than the benefit of a clean kitchen. Your child is likely to obey you the next time she goes out to play not because she wants to or sees the need to, but because she is afraid of being punished. Psychologically, she learns that power gives you confidence while she should be learning to trust her creativity and have faith in her ability.

To prove that punishment does more harm than good, Ivan Pavlov, a Russian psychologist conducted a social experiment. Every time he fed his dog, he noticed that the dog salivated. In his investigation, Pavlov rang a bell whenever he gave his dog food.

He repeated this many times and then took away the food, and rang the bell on its own. From his study, Pavlov noted that when the bell rang, and the dog received no food, salivation increased.

Charles Duhigg in his book "The Power of Habit: Why We Do What We Do in Life and Business," states that to form habits or behavior patterns you see a cue, follow a routine and get a reward.

In Pavlov's experience, his dog learned to associate the bell (cue) with the food (routine) and satisfaction (reward). This habit, or behavior, is classical conditioning.

If then a dog can associate a bell with food, it is only natural to assume that using a negative consequence and associating it with undesired behavior, will result to the desired behavior due to fear of the negative consequence.

Punishment tends to make children feel bad about themselves and others. Your child concludes that they are treated so harshly because they are bad; they cannot do anything right and deserve what is coming to them. Moreover, since they are not good, it is only natural that they behave in a way that gets them punished.

Duhigg explains that if the cue, routine, reward loop is repeated enough times, the brain goes to automatic setting and will naturally follow the habit loop when a cue is presented. When a parent uses punishment or discipline to correct a child, a habit loop is formed in the child's brain, in this case, a negative loop.

If you are fond of using punishment and your child never cooperates, the reason could be that the habit has already been engraved in their brain. Your child already knows that the consequence of their bad behavior will be punished and since they already believe (or are starting to feel) that they are bad, a vicious cycle will form.

So, they get into more trouble, and the punishment they receive affirms their behavior, and it becomes their default settings.

Discipline, on the other hand, is the complete opposite of punishment. Parents who use positive discipline work first on controlling their emotions, and respond to their children in a calm, rational way. It takes time to master so don't feel bad if you are not yet there.

For instance, in our previous example, you would have first thought of why your little girl came running to the kitchen and is pulling you towards the yard. She must be over the moon that she has learned to plant a seed and wants to show off. We all want to show off when we do something great.

Instead of scolding her for the mud and mess, the best alternative would be first to see her planted seed. Once her excitement has dropped a notch, you can walk with her to the kitchen and explain why rushing in without considering the hard work you put into cleaning the kitchen is not cool. You will notice that she will nod in understanding as her brain makes all the connection. Do not be surprised if she apologizes and is open to help you clean the mess before she takes a bath.

Using Pavlov's experiment, we can conclude that, naturally, a positive response to an undesired behavior will result in the desired behavior due to understanding and respect.

The difference between punishment and discipline is that, although both methods get the job done, the resulting behavior and mental attitude will differ significantly: the latter will nurture respect and understanding while the former instills fear of consequence.

Chapter 2: The Main Goals of Discipline

Parenting is rewarding when everyone, especially your children, is cooperating. It is valuable, but it can also be stressful. Pre-schoolers and toddlers are curious, ambitious, fearless, and know nothing about safety. This development curiosity is more often the beginning of mischief and misbehavior. Children don't understand the importance of behaving in a certain way.

The goal of positive parenting and discipline is to develop self-control and problem-solving skills for an all-around child. When a child misbehaves, you want them to stop immediately (short term goal) and never repeat the behavior in question (long term goal). It is understandable why most parents use threats and punishment for both short term and long-term discipline goals.

Positive discipline involves making a conscious decision based on pre-determined principles you have thought about and agreed on. With this approach, you meet the short-term discipline goals of clear boundaries and the long-term goal of teaching life skills, without affecting the development of your child in a negative way.

Let's say, for example, your two-year-old, Joyanne throws a temper-tantrum. She wants you to play tea party with her, but you have explained you will join her as soon as you shoot a quick email about something urgent.

She does not understand what is more urgent than a tea party, so she hits you. Most parents will grab the little girl by the hand and sternly warn her that it is not okay to, hit people. Parents may go a step further and give her time-out as a consequence for her misbehavior.

Is this the worst approach? No, it's not. Could it be better!

What you need is a clear roadmap that leads to what you want to achieve when your child misbehaves. Discipline is meant to train. If you dish out rules and give consequences without explanations or considerations, you are achieving very little in teaching behavior but accomplishing much in instilling fear.

The short-term goal of any parent is to get their child to stop misbehaving immediately. In a restaurant setting, you want your child to sit still, order for their meal, eat in peace and have dessert without a fuss. However, with kids, this is unlikely. What do you do when they reach for your friend's cutlery and insists they want your friend's dessert instead? You want your child to stop embarrassing you and eat their dessert using their cutlery. To achieve this, you can either use a threat which will instantly have them stop or use your discipline road map.

By telling your child that you will not go out with them again, you expect that they will weigh the option of being left behind because of misbehavior and immediately fall in line. However, children's rational thoughts are not developed enough to understand this. Your child is likely to feel threatened, hurt, unloved and their choices ignored as opposed to thinking of why they would not want to be left behind during an outing.

A mother once found herself in this situation. While her friend did not mind the little boy using her cutlery or eating her dessert, the mother was determined to use the incident to teach her son how to treat other people and respect boundaries. She politely asked him if he wanted to use a different set of cutleries to which the boy responded yes. She then asked him what he would do if someone snatched his favorite toy car making him think about the other person's feelings and understand that taking other people's things was not okay. He should instead ask politely and request to switch his dessert.

According to Daniel J. Siegel, M.d and Tina Payne Bryson, Ph. D in their book "No Drama Discipline: Whole-Brain Way to Calm the Chaos and Nature Your Child Developing Brain," there are three fundamental questions every positive parent must ask themselves when a child misbehaves.

1. Why did my child act this way?

Using curiosity rather than anger, you can deduce the reason behind your child's misbehavior. Children find it difficult to communicate complex emotions such as anger and frustrations. That is why they will hit you when you can't play tea party when they demand it or throw a tantrum when they can't have a fifth scoop of ice cream.

2. What lesson do I want to teach?

Depending on the situation, you will want to teach your child responsibility, sharing, caring for others, patience and many other lessons. For example, when she hits you because she wants to play tea party, you can use the opportunity to teach tolerance through delayed gratifications.

3. How can I best teach this lesson?

There is no one size fit all for this question. Consider your child's developmental stage, the context of the situation and device a smart way to communicate what you want to teach. Children enjoy role play and using it to teach them life lessons will help them understand quickly and respond positively. When a child is angry or hurt, it is natural that they will not want to apologize immediately they misbehave. Using role-play, you can quickly calm them down and make them more receptive to an apology.

Using these three questions, -why, what and how- you can quickly change your child's behavior in the short term and lay a strong foundation for their decision-making skills for the future. We want our children to make sound decisions in our absence.

Using Duhigg's principle on how habits emerge, positive parenting becomes your autopilot discipline habit. Your child misbehaves (cue) you use your definite discipline roadmap -why what, how- (routine) your child stops misbehaving (rewards).

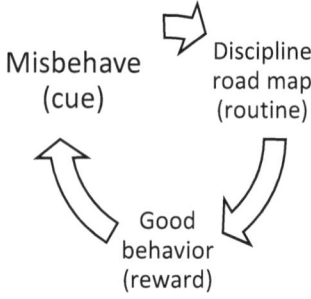

Misbehave (cue)

Discipline road map (routine)

Good behavior (reward)

Your child uses the same principle to learn skills. He misbehaves (cue) you use your definite discipline roadmap (routine) he learns an essential skill (rewards). With time, indiscipline reduces as your child learns new skills and recalls them whenever he needs to ask you for something.

Toddlers and preschoolers forget and sometimes disregard lessons we teach them. At this stage, retaining information is not as easy as with an adult. Even adults do disregard lessons from time to time.

For a habit to form, the aspect of repetition is crucial. Keep repeating the lesson more often, and your child will soon recall it on autopilot. It is tempting to get back to the old blueprint, punishment, especially when you have repeated the lesson so many times. Your child is testing your limits, which is not a bad thing. By showing her that you are not relenting, she will follow your lead and use the lesson you taught. Children do not test us because they are spoilt brats.

When you leave your child with someone else for a few hours, your child is usually well behaved. According to research, this difference is significant because of the level of comfort your child feels when they are around you. While this is not an excuse to misbehave, children test us because they feel safe around us. They are comfortable, and whether they know it or not, it is a perfect learning ground for them. As they move through development stages and you learn to use your discipline roadmap, children become well behaved even in their parent's presence.

Chapter 3: How it Worked Before

Disciplining children is not a recent controversy. Since time immemorial, parents have been devising ways to keep their children in line. In 1600 through to 1800, parents used what is now called the Puritan discipline method.

Strict corporal punishment was a popular form of discipline, derived from the Old Testament. Proverbs 29:15 "A rod and a reprimand impart wisdom, but a child left undisciplined disgraces its mother" was used as the basis of punishment. Harsh punishment was common in society and homes discouraged children against rebellion to authority. The slightest provocation was enough to whip a child.

Children were expected to be well-behaved, a reflection of their parents. With religion playing a significant role in how children were viewed, parents were under constant pressure to punish their children into acting accordingly. Phrases such as "spare the rod spoil the child" and "a child left to himself bringeth his mother shame" were commonly used to rebuke parents who did not comply with the acceptable mode of punishment.

Puritan children learned that rebellion and challenging their parent was forcing God to condemn them to eternal judgment where they would burn in fire and brimstone. The strict punishment, through physical abuse, would bring them atonement.

Scenes of children being whipped in public and being forced to make public confessions at meetings were common as stated in the research Journal of Children and Family Studies. Children were made to feel guilty for their actions. They were threatened continuously and were believed to have no autonomy. Besides being threatened with the eternal punishment of the soul, children were thought to be born arrogant and needing strict discipline started at an early age to shape them.

Not everyone was pro-punishment. John Locke, an English physician, wrote parenting guides that formed the basis of the positive discipline methods used today. Although his guides were not popular, Locke presented that children resembled a blank table when they were born and were not predisposed to sin.

Throughout the 17th century, Locke encouraged parents to allow children to learn consequences naturally which build self-control and a desire to own their action through guidance. Locke, who was later named the father of liberalism, strongly opposed harsh punishment with his message.

In the 1900s, child-rearing experts proposed new methods of forcing children into good behavior. A popular way introduced during this time was the scorecard. A scorecard was posted at home and in school with duties and responsibilities a child was to fulfill. "Rising on time, writing to grandma, finishing homework, eating all their food" are everyday duties children are expected to perform. A gold start would be given when the child performed their duties while a black mark would be used when the child failed to do so. Rewards and punishment were then assigned following the scorecard's guidance. Also, children during this time were expected to stand whenever an adult entered a room. During a bus ride, children were to give up their seat and their place in line for a bus. At school, boys got spanking for indiscipline while girls were slapped on the knuckles.

The increase in research and philosophies in child rearing brought with it its fair share of confusion for parents. Religion still held a fundamental part in their lives, and parents often became confused between following philosophies and their pastors.

Child rearing philosophies had its shortcomings. They presented conflicting messages on how much permissiveness should be allowed versus how much punishment was to be used. Some theories offered strict rules to form proper eating habits, sleeping patterns, and social tendencies, while others preferred a more gentle means.

Disciplining a child does not require following standards set by status quo. This is the message Dr. Spoke used to encourage parents to trust their instincts in the mid-1950s. By telling parents, "you know more than you think" in his first publication of Baby and Child Care, Spoke advocated for being reasonable, friendly, open and consistent with kids as an epitome for building relationships with other people as opposed to punishment.

Spokes' principle of raising children results in the rebellious teens of the 1960s and 1970s. His beliefs were rebuked by the strict experts who encouraged authoritarian parenting style. A clear demarcation was drawn between parents who spank and non-spanking parents, a divide that is still evident today. According to research, only 19% of parents in the United States believe in positive discipline.

Looking back at this style of discipline, the punishment adults inflicted on children were unfair and unnecessary. To an elderly who looks back at what life was back then, the society is immoral and disrespectful.

With technology advancement where kids can spend hours playing violent video games, positive discipline is needed now more than ever. To strike a right balance would mean, picking the "good" parts that made children in the 50's so disciplined and combining it with the elimination of negative child influence found today.

Chapter 4: What is Positive Discipline

You are sited at the dinner table, and you pour gravy on your three-year-old's turkey. As luck would have it, she wanted to pour the gravy herself. Because children are clumsy by nature, you defiantly poured the gravy amidst her request. What follows is a temper tantrum, screaming and throwing hands in the air, pushing the turkey away and crying for what seems like hours. You try your best to calm her down, but she will not have it. Soon, everyone on the table is contributing, some accusing your little girl of spoiling dinner for everyone.

After a long day at work tackling that impossible task, getting held up in traffic for hours and finally managing to cook dinner, you are tempted to shout, "Stop it right now." Are sounds familiar, does it?

Our forefathers had two main responses when faced with danger, fight or flee. Walter Cannon first described this response in the 1920s. Cannon realized a chemical reaction in our body that mobilizes resources within us and helps us deal with threatening situations. Today, this theory is described as a stress response.

A stressful situation such as the probability of losing your job, a group of people running behind you in a dark alley and a looming deadline can trigger this chemical reaction. The fight-or-flight response is a survival mechanism and helps you to either fight or flee for dear life. While this is great for life-threatening situations, the body often overreacts to stressors that are not life-threatening. Work pressure, traffic jams and family challenges are among the most common stressors. No wonder you are not able to keep it together after a long day when your child throws a tantrum!

The natural reaction would be to fight which is exactly what most parents do when they shout "stop it right now." While a discipline challenge can easily make you go into fight-or-flight mode, you do not have to let it take over. This is where positive parenting comes in.

Remember your child is also in fight-or-flight mode. They wanted to pour gravy on the turkey, and now they are angry you did not let them. They are fighting for what they want. Positive parenting is minimizing the child's frustration and reducing undesired behavior. Instead of punishing bad behavior, positive parenting advocates for creatively modeling and teaching children positive behavior. You approach your child with love, empathy, respect, and kindness and use gentle or loving guidance to explain the desired behavior.

Before attempting to discipline your child, take a step back and put yourself in their shoes. When you were three years old, you went through the same uncontrolled emotions. How your parents reacted to your emotional outburst, their parenting and discipline style made you who are today. It is likely that the reaction you are having right now is the same one your parents had. Think about it. How did that make you feel? History always repeats itself. Research has shown that how we parent our children will be influenced by how our parents raised us. Everyone was wounded as a child. Healing these wounds enables us to parent our children as we want.

Chapter 5: Positive discipline and your child's development

For the longest time, you have told your nine-year-old to make their bed in the morning, but they seem to forget all the time. As you do the occasional rounds to their room to pick laundry, you notice that he made his bed. You smile, pleased that he finally remembered and secretly hope the trend continues. The bed needs a little straightening here and there, but it's straightened nonetheless. There are no toys on the floor, and the room is surprisingly neat. You promise to mention it during dinner and cook him his favorite meal.

After making his bed two days in a row, you walk in to find the occasional mess you were hoping to forget. You sigh and go about your business cleaning, picking up toys and making the bed. Because you have an early morning, your son is still in the kitchen eating breakfast, and you are tempted to march him to his room to clean up before he goes, but should do you do?

Before we answer that, let us take a closer look at children and how they develop.

Raising children is like traveling on an airplane. When trouble occurs, parents are advised to wear their gas masks first and then help their children because children are vulnerable. If you cannot trust children with a gas mask, how about controlling their emotions and actions?

Because of their lack of control, children rely on us to model the way they should behave. Imagine then, the picture we create when we march downstairs guns blazing and march them to their room for not cleaning up. This is not how we would want them to react when someone else did not fulfill their end of the bargain, yet, it is precisely what we are modeling.

When your child forgets to make his bed, you can use the why, what, how model to remind him of his duty without making him feel guilty he forgot to do it. Could he have woken up extremely hungry today and filling his stomach was his priority this morning? Alternatively, maybe his mind was occupied by something else, and he genuinely forgot about the bed.

As you go back to the kitchen to speak with your son, let us consider positive parenting and emotional development in kids.

Positive Parenting and Emotional development in Kids

When using positive parenting, you share your emotions openly with your child which in turn helps them understand where you are coming from. For instance, during water play at the park, your child may shove another kid and make them cry or rush across a slippery floor carelessly. Instead of embarrassing them in front of other kids, you can talk to your kid about why shoving another child made them cry. However, just before we get to that part, first ask your child why he felt he needed to push the other child. Maybe the other child had a toy he wanted to play with but won't share, making your child jealous and angry. This would explain why your child shoved him and give you a better ground on handling the situation. Jealousy is a complex emotion, and your child may not know how to handle it yet.

In this scenario, the first step would be empathizing with your child's emotions. This helps your child calm down and engage their rational side of the brain, make sense and understand what is happening.

To help them further, name the feeling. Your child is likely to recognize the feeling next time he feels it and may even mention it to you. Also and most importantly, your child will feel a little stronger next time he is handling a strong emotion instead of letting it sweep over him.

"You feel a little angry that he does not want to share, don't you? And a little jealous of him too?"

An effective way of handling emotional situations is to use stories that are relatable to our kids. Anger and jealousy will keep cropping up before your child can control and overcome them. There must have been a similar situation that happened a while back you can use to correct the behavior.

"Well, remember the time your little sister wanted to play with your toy car, and you wanted to play with it too? You did feel a little angry like today didn't you? But allowing her to play with it first gave you a chance to play with it longer right?"

You can use the same principle when your child runs across a slippery floor. Tell them how that made you feel as a parent and explain why it is not good. If an accident had occurred to them, or someone they know, use that story to illustrate the danger and repercussions.

Whether we are aware of it or not, we are continually coaching our children on how to handle emotions. How we interact with our kids helps them process their feelings and those of people around them. Building their emotional intelligence helps our child learn how to:

- Self-sooth
- Have emotional self-awareness and acceptance
- Control their impulses
- Be empathetic

Emotions are a core part of human development, and while many parents find it complicated, it is essential that we embrace this responsibility. Emotions matter and when children can control their emotions, they can control their behavior.

Let's think about our own emotions for a minute. You will not take on a big project at work if you are anxious, you will not start your own business if you are afraid and again you will not solve a conflict with a friend, your spouse or a co-worker if you can't understand their perspective and manage your anger. Your ability to handle your emotions determines the quality of your life, which makes it crucial to teach children how to handle and manage their emotions.

0-13 months of emotional development
At 0-13 months, a baby's developmental task is to learn how to trust. They can pick up anxieties (fear)

from you or feel reassured, by your tone or voice, your touch and movement. When a baby's stress hormones shoot up, from TV, loud noises and angry voices, your loving arms, kind eyes, and secure cuddling will make them feel better and trust that things are ok.

Building trust brings self-soothing, intimate connection and happy moods for kids making it paramount to provide reassurance as regularly as possible. Luckily, your baby's crying drives you crazy, and you are more likely to pick him up and soothe him.

Over the years, parents had been advised that babies learn to self-soothe when you leave them to cry. Scientists, however, claim that just like an adult, constant exposure to stress in babies leads to increased heart rate, reduce oxygen levels and an increase in stress hormones.

Instead of wiring the developing brain of your baby that he is safe, your baby's brain becomes wired for fight-or-flight. When a baby is left to cry, he eventually falls asleep not from self-soothing, but exhaustion. Eventually, he learns that his parents will not respond and asking for help is futile.

A parent who leaves their baby to cry is also likely to find parenting hard. Every time the baby cries and you ignore, you diminish your inbuilt empathy for your baby that enables you to see things from your baby's point of view. This is the first sure step in disconnecting with your baby

It is impossible to soothe your baby every time they are upset, but nature has taken care of this. As you respond and soothe your baby, his body produces a hormone called oxytocin in response to your loving attention. As he releases oxytocin, more oxytocin receptors are produced which help him feel good and calm himself in your absence. This is the hormone responsible for self-soothing, and more it is produced, the easier it is for your child to self-soothe.

So, when your little girl is screaming her head off because she wanted to pour the gravy, the best thing you can do is first sooth her. Take her on your lap and soothe her, allow her to express her disappointment and to feel it. Once her hormones balance and she is calm, explain to her why you preferred to pour the gravy. She will feel loved and safe and understand that your intention was not to hurt her.

This is the same safety and trust she felt when she was young and had no idea gravy existed. Your kind words, loving cuddle, and comfort will reassure her. Everyone will win and have a great dinner.

13-36 months Toddlers emotional development

Toddler years are probably the most challenging in human development for both parent and child. If you have been soothing your child when they cry, then you already have a head start in coping with the challenges you will face when your little one is 13-36 months old.

During this development stage, your toddler wants to assert herself and feel that she has an impact on the world and control over her experiences. She is also learning how to love herself, form her own opinions and pronounce them. Your little girl will start to advocate for her desire which many parents are not prepared for.

A curious toddler will often touch anything that arouses her curiosity as they try to figure out what it is and what it does. Many parents find themselves at loggerheads with their kids. Parents see themselves giving warnings and threats more often than they would like to.

"Don't touch that. Slow down you will hurt yourself. Get down from there. No! Would you be still while I change you? We don't hit people."

And the tantrums will start, from throwing herself on the floor to screaming and more biting and hitting. Parents have been told to ignore tantrums and not reward children when they throw a fit. But the child sees it from a very different perspective. To her, the parents who would rush to comfort her and help when she was stressed as a child have now abandoned her. She has no idea who they are. In all honesty, parents mean well when they do this. They are teaching their children independence and responsibility through discipline. What most parents do not realize is that ignoring their children causes a relationship to disconnect in the relationship they worked so hard to build when their toddlers were babies.

Toddlers can't differentiate between their emotions and behavior and will conclude that they are bad. She interprets that if she does what she wants, she is bad and so, to be loved and accepted she must do what her parents want. This build into repressed shame that can shadow her for the rest of her life.

Toddlers have a lot to deal with in their daily life. They build stress hormones as adults do, but since their intellect is not well developed, they cannot talk it out, work out to release the pressure or rationalize their emotions. So, nature created a way out for them, tantrums. Tantrums help toddlers release emotions and regain equilibrium. Parents make the understandable mistake that tantrums are within their toddlers' control and fail to give their little ones what they need most.

Toddlers don't enjoy tantrums, they would prefer to feel cherished and loved than to throw a fit. Parents have always responded to outbursts using punishment, either threatening the child or ignoring them. While this stops the outburst, it creates deep insecurity in your child that by expressing themselves, you may even abandon them, no wonder they become aggressive, whiny, clingy preschoolers.

Just like toddlers, seating with your child during a tantrum helps them self-soothe and control their emotions. A parent who stays with their child as they tantrum reassures the child that they live in a warm, safe, and loving place. They realize that the universe is friendly and they are accepted.

Through our guidance, children can follow essential rules that will help them get along with others. In the meantime, we must have the patience to deal with their extreme emotional outbursts. We should not allow our toddlers to act upon all their emotions. For instance, being angry and jealous that the other boy is playing with the truck is not a reason to push him. We have to set guidelines on what is acceptable behavior and limit destructive behavior.

Preschoolers (3-5 years) Emotional Development

You are at a family function with your preschooler. You are happy they are finally in school, and the teacher can help deal with the tantrums they continue to throw every so often. One of your nieces starts to cry and her cousins, including your preschooler, go to comfort him. You hear your little boy shouting to his crying cousin, "Shut up! You are hurting my ears. Alternatively, you are a big girl; you can't keep crying like a baby." Statements he hears you tell him whenever he throws a fit.

This is a common occurrence with children who have learned to suppress their feelings. The baby who was never soothing as an infant reacts easily and throws a tantrum now and then. His parents mean well but are ill-informed and often threaten him with abandonment, so, his radar is always looking out for danger, just in case they make true their threat.

His parents know they will never leave their child, but he does not know that, neither does he have the capacity to process it. He stays on guard twenty-four seven. He is needy and demanding because that is the only way his parents listen to him and not all the time, only when they have had enough of the nagging and tantrums.

He tries to keep his feelings at bay because he has concluded that his parents will not help him with his emotional struggle. But because he is a child and cannot control his emotions very well, he fails miserably at suppressing his feelings which only gets him in trouble because his parents send him for time out to "think about what he has done."

When he sees his cousin crying, he can't take it because his relationship model says that people should suppress their emotions. Thus, he shouts at his cousin to shut up. Some kids wall themselves so much that other people's hurt feelings do not evoke empathy in them.

Preschoolers emotional development stage is learning to be empathetic. When a baby hears another baby cry, he begins to cry as well. Empathy is inbuilt in mammals, we naturally feel what other people are feeling, and we are compelled to help them or look for a way they can receive help.

As the little girl continues to cry, her other cousin pulls her into a warm hug and soothes her, telling her that everything will be okay. When babies receive empathy at a young age, it lays a foundation for them to show compassion to other people. Such a child is comfortable with feelings because she has experienced them at one time or another. The warm embrace from her father reassures her that she will be fine and after she regained her equilibrium, she realizes that it was not so bad, she was fine.

When she sees another child crying, she will naturally handle the situation the way her parents have handled it with her. If she is unable to soothe the crying child, she will call for help. She understands her emotions and can recognize them in other people.

By the time a child starts pre-school, his brain is mature enough to evaluate if a given response is acceptable or not. He still needs comfort from you, but he has learned to self-soothe and use his words to describe how he is feeling instead of throwing a tantrum.

He is likely to wait his turn instead of aggressively pushing other kids so he can go first. He will control himself when he wants a toy another child is playing with and will be the one wiping tears off another child's cheek and trying to cheer them up.

This emotional self-awareness shows that his left-side of the brain (his logical part of the brain) is integrating with his right side of the brain (his emotional side).

6-10 years of elementary schoolers emotional development
By the time a child is six years, their nervous system is almost entirely wired, their logical brain strengthens and can organize and prune thoughts and emotion. They are more organized, can plan and have a steadier self-control mechanism.

According to research, the brain of a six-year-old has the potential to adapt and change. To some extent, it can be retrained. They have built the basic of self-soothing, ability to trust and empathize. They have already concluded how relationships work, based on their experiences. Elementary schoolers have created strategies to deal with their feelings.

The boy who is not sure if they can trust their parents may be more stable emotionally, but he will occasionally have emotional outbursts easily. They are more fragile than they look and will often replace tantrums with sulking and banging the door behind them as they lock themselves in their room.

Children who have grown up in positive parenting home can regulate their own emotions and can control them most of the time. They are in charge of their behavior, and their neurology is built to deliver self-soothing chemicals and regulate fear and anger response. They use their full brain power to function, feel comfortable in their skin and with other people's emotions and forming deep human connections easily.

Children encounter many challenges as they develop in a fast-changing world. Elementary schoolers put their emotions to work as they go through these challenges and use it as an opportunity to mature in their emotional intelligence. They pick up cues that cause triggers and store them in their brain to use when a similar situation occurs in the future.

Children with low emotional intelligence have difficulty picking up cues. They have trouble mastering and navigating everyday development task which makes their self-esteem suffer. Unlike their counterparts, children with low emotional intelligence find it challenging to negotiate anger and anxiety and cower from taking on responsibilities.

Because of the maturity that comes with age, children in this development stage do not need their parents as much as they did before which is a sign of relief to parents. They struggle with their emotions internally, but this does not mean that elementary schoolers don't need guidance.

Children at this age easily communicate their feelings and have a full grasp of what is happening to them. It is the best time for parents to help their children master their emotions to full capacity by talking things out and reasoning with their soon to be teens. Parents can teach their children problem-solving skills and reflections by brainstorming on the options available.

Now let's go back to the nine-year-old who forgot to make his bed and often leaves a mess every day. How do we use positive discipline to change his behavior?

If he has a constant outburst of emotions, it is safe to conclude that his emotional intelligence is still low and he may need a little more love and care than his counterpart with high emotional intelligence. Instead of punishing him or making him feel bad he forgot to clean up his room, a better approach would be to have a conversation about it and look at the options available. If he finds that he gets late whenever he makes his bed and picks up toys in the morning, you can work out strategies to minimize this workload. For instance, sleeping after picking up toys would give him enough time to make his bed in the morning. Also, sleeping half an hour early would mean more rest and a burst of new energy in the morning. He would be more prepared to make his bed and prepare for school.

Is it too late for the child who has grown up with low emotional intelligence? Not! While it is harder to change the brain wiring of an older child, it is possible. It will take patience, love, and guidance, just like a toddler. You will need to validate her action so that she learns how to trust you and to believe in herself.

Let us consider how to help your emotionally sensitive elementary schooler.

It's the weekend. You are helping your elementary schooler with homework; she keeps rubbing her work and changing the topic. She does not want to do her homework, and you can see it written all over her. You give her a pass and allow her to play for a few hours hoping her mind will settle down into doing her homework later on.

By evening, she is complaining that her teacher gave her too much work for the weekend. She complains that the work is challenging and she cannot comprehend it. You look at her book only to notice it is something she has done before. She knows the answers; she doesn't want to do her homework. She tries to keep it together as you have always asked her to but the stress emotions bottling up build too quickly and waterfalls follow.

Because of the use of punishment, you can see her insecurity as she fights to keep it together. She is suppressing her emotions because that is the relationship model she has learned. If you look closely at her, you can see her struggle to keep it together amid the tears, hoping and praying that you do not reprimand and send her to her room.

Generally, children by this age would be able to control their emotions, and that's where the challenge is. An ill-informed parent will punish the child and solidify further the child's insecurities, but as parents learn positive parenting, helping this little girl will take a different route.

The toddler and the preschooler learned to trust by being allowed to feel their emotions. They were taught how to identify and name their feelings and when they were calm, they learned how to handle their feelings through the pep talk their parents gave.

Your elementary schooler has learned to name her emotions though she cannot control them well enough. By getting a meltdown during homework, the best you can do is hug and allow her to calm down just as you would to a smaller child. Once she is calm, talk about why she is finding her homework difficult and ask her to give options for how she would like to handle her homework once you settle on a plan, action it out.

Your preschooler starts learning how to trust you with her emotions. It will take some time for them to open up entirely because she still has her sensor on guard, just in case this is a drill. Give her some time, as trust builds, you will see an enormous change in her behavior and her emotional control.

She will not always need discipline. A single mom was telling me how she had had a rough day at work one day. She was so tired that she slept throughout the morning. Her elementary schooler was up before her and busied herself with toasting bread and attempted to make some tea using the kettle.

Was the kitchen messy? As messy as a child can make it, but breakfast was delicious. Her child was being thoughtful and making breakfast for her tired mom was the best way she knew she would help out. From the stresses of last night, her mom would have decided to scold her for the messy kitchen, completely ignoring her child's kind gesture. What if something blew up and started a fire?

Instead, she validated her child's action by hugging her and thanking her for making breakfast, ignoring the mess in the kitchen. Once they were done with breakfast, her daughter helped her clean up the kitchen, and she told her that making breakfast was great, but she would prefer it if she were present just in case something went wrong and her daughter needed help. At least until she was sure, her daughter could handle simple kitchen appliances without her help.

By validating her daughters' actions and warning her of the danger she unknowingly put herself in, she built her daughters' self-esteem and used the opportunity to teach her responsibilities. As an elementary schooler continues to be validated and helped to handle emotions, she soon builds her emotional intelligence and handles herself and her behavior without feeling overwhelmed.

Positive discipline and brain development

You passed by the store today and picked up two toys for your kids. One gets a red teddy and the other a green teddy. When you get home, you are excited to show your kids their presents. The pair runs down when you walk in excited that you are finally back. You place the shopping on the kitchen table and excitedly exclaim that you have presents for everyone.

"What did you get me?" the girls ask impatiently. You remove the green teddy and hand it to one girl and then the red teddy to the other girl. Suddenly, there is a problem.

"No! It's not fair. No." cries one of your girls. You dumbfounded, and all you can think about is, 'what just happened.'

"What's wrong sweetie?" you ask.

"I wanted the green one. I always get the red one." She cries.

It has been a custom of yours to get the girls toys in green and red (each their favorite color). It looks like things have changed. What do you do?

To understand how to handle this situation best, let us first understand how the human brain works, more so how a child's brain develops.

When a child is born, they already have a lot of the neurons they will need for the rest of their lives. The brain of a child is 25% the size of an adult brain. Early in their life, children form a lot more synapsis, electrical signals that connect neurons and send messages to and from the brain, than they need. Although not all neurons will make it to adulthood, they allow children to learn things faster than adults do.

Your child naturally fuels the formation of this synapses and decides which one is important and which ones are not by the nurture they receive from you. A synapse strengthens the more it is used. Synapses are made strong through the formation of ideas in the brain and through learning a set of skills.

The things that children often use like walking and language stay ingrained in the child's brain. Because this is the point your child is creating synapses, it is the perfect time to learn skills, including behavior. This is why, how you discipline your child at this stage matters a lot. You want them to keep the skills that will help them throughout their life and prune the ones that will get them into trouble, hurt others and leave them in despair.

The neurologist believes that the brain has three main regions:

The Reptilian brain made up of the limbic area and brain stem. This part of the brain is responsible for your child's bodily function such as breathing, heartbeat, digestion and more complex functions like survival.

The mammalian brain is the emotional brain. It is responsible for strong emotions like anger, frustration, love, rage, fear, anxiety, caring and nurturing. This is what took over when the little girl did not want the red teddy. The reptilian brain and the mammalian brain are also called the lower mind. It is the lower part of the brain that causes your little one to shove another kid when he wants a toy and to hit you when you don't give him the attention he seeks.

The human brain also called the thinking mind, is responsible for learning, reasoning, logic, problem-solving, flexibility, and adaptability, morality, empathy, sophisticated thinking and decision making. This part of the brain helps us live happy, balanced lives and develop meaningful relationships. The very qualities we want to build in our children.

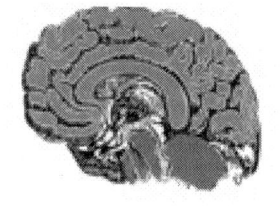

Thinking Brain

Mammalian Brain

Reptilian Brain

These skills require your child to have a well-developed thinking brain, which is where discipline comes in to help guide a child's mind on how to pay attention, think, make decisions, solve problems and also how to interact with others.

The human brain develops fully around age twenty-six. In the meantime, learning and re-learning is the order of the day. As parent's, we need to adjust our expectation when it comes to the behavior of our children. If the part of the brain responsible for reliable functioning logic, emotional balance and morality will take twenty-six years to develop, it is only logical to assume that kids will be kids.

They will forget their homework at school, occasionally hit you (or throw a tantrum) to get attention and forget to pick up toys when you have said it a thousand times before. The good thing is, this will not happen all the time. As they practice the skill, their synapses become stronger, and they remember to perform their 'responsibilities' more often.

A developing brain changes every day. To illustrate, let us consider the right temporals parietal junction (TPJ), a part of the thinking brain. When you put yourself in another person's shoes, you engage your TPJ and view the situation from the other person's point of view.

The developing brain of a child will be unable to consider motives and intentions, making it difficult for them to make sound decisions when faced with a problem. For example, the fact that red is the little girls favorite color and that is why you brought her a red teddy is irrelevant. To her, getting a red toy all the time is unfair.

Our work as parents is to put ourselves in our kid's shoes and see a situation from their perspective before we decide on how to solve the problem. Putting ourselves in their shoes will teach our children to use their TPJ when handling other people.

"You don't like the teddy?" the mother might ask her little girl.

"NO!" she shoots the answer.

If the mother engaged her TPJ, she would know that her daughter does not mean it. She likes the teddy but is not pleased with the color.

At this point, the little girl has already engaged her reptilian brain and is demonstrating strong emotions (frustration, anger, and sadness). Her mother can either escalate the situation or engage the thinking mind of her daughter.

"Well, I'll take it back if you don't want it. You should appreciate that I took the time to buy you the teddy, all you do is complain instead? Give it to your sister; she seems to like toys better than you do, ungrateful little ¬¬……."

Yelling, a form of punishment engages the reptilian brain and only escalates the issue. When the reptilian brain is online, the thinking brain shuts down. In our example, the little girl may throw the teddy on the floor and start a fight with her sister for the red teddy. She may even step on the teddy.

What is fascinating about the brain is that the thinking part of the brain has soothing strands that can calm the reptilian brain when it is reactive. By naming the emotions a child is experiencing, you tame the reptilian brain and engage the thinking mind, soothing the child. Synapses become strong when they are engaged continuously, so by training your child to activate her thinking brain in a stressful situation. You reinforce her synapses preparing her to calm the storm and reflect in harsh conditions.

So, when the little girl melts down over a green teddy, the mother is better equipped if she lets her calm down first by pulling her into an embrace and when there is a deep sigh, you know that the reptilian brain has been sent offline bringing the thinking mind back online. The mother can then take her through the reasons why she chose to give her a red teddy and not a green one. But because the little girl cannot use logic at this time, this approach will probably not bear any fruit, and her daughter will insist that she wants the green teddy.

By remaining calm and empathetic, the mother can explain that her sister will play with her and share the green teddy. On the next trip to the store, she will get a green toy and try mixing up colors, so that they may have toyed with a wide range of colors.

After presenting all this information, the little girl may still be adamant on getting the green teddy, and that's okay. Positive parenting does not always end in roses and rainbows. Our role as parents is to be empathetic and remain calm, once you have explained that she cannot instantly get the green teddy, you can hold her as she completely calms down and joins her sister to play or distract her with something else that will cheer her up.

Positive parenting does not guarantee that you will always get the results you hoped for, what it will do is lower the explosive emotions, reduce the tantrums and avoid any harm that would have resulted from using force and punishment to calm the situation.

The most important thing to remember is that kids are human beings. They have their desires, emotions, and agendas that they are willing to defend. Positive parenting is about being there for our kids and being there with them when they go through a distressing situation. Letting them know that we won't reject or turn our backs on them even when they are at their worst.

Kids, in turn, feel safe and learn to express themselves and develop into independent thinkers able to think through situations, comprehend their emotions and consider other people's perspectives before making a decision.

So, positive parenting helps develop the brain of a child. It strengthens their neurons which make it easy for them to connect their thinking and reptile brain. These leads to personal insight, responsibility, flexibility, empathy, morality, and sound decision making.

Chapter 6: The basics of positive discipline

Connect with your child
Knowing that you are on their side, is what allows your child to risk, learn, grow and be resilient. It is also the secret to being a happy parent. Children do not like commands, but it is impossible not to use commands when we cannot connect with our kids.

To connect with children, parents need to regulate their emotions by healing their wounds. A child's indiscipline does not cause the anger or anxiety that lead to a constant power struggle, fear, and doubt. Our experiences as children do. The tantrum we caused is part of who we are, and they take charge whenever we are upset by the environment we are in.

Our children particularly have a way of triggering these unhappy feelings. We see ourselves in them and the vulnerability we had when we were kids, and we want to do better. But the painful past sometimes overtakes us, and we end up inflicting the same unpleasant experiences on our children. We mean well, but the hard wiring of our neurons on relationships fail us.

For us, disciplining with love is a foreign concept, and we can't grasp it, at least not yet. By learning to look within and work on our insecurities, we can offer our children the secure foundation that will provide them the foundation necessary to form lasting relationships.

Our deepest fear is to raise unhappy children whom nobody wants to associate with. We fear this so much that we end up being too hard on kids during discipline, to keep them in line and avoid the sharks of loneliness and disappointment. But since we cannot control what happens to our kids, our jobs is to help them build a foundation that allows them to surround themselves with people who will accept them and help them find deep meaning in their lives.

We want to raise children who can control their behavior because they are easy to live with. We wish to rear successful children, not necessarily as society perceives success, but in discovering, honoring and sharing their unique gifts with others. To do this, we must learn to manage our anxieties and give our children the necessary space to discover who they are, build confidence and resilience in themselves.

Dealing with the past

To deal with our childhood anxieties and be the parents we want to be for our kids, we need to parent consciously. Pay attention to when kids push our buttons and note it down. Whenever we feel triggered, we stumble on something that needs to be healed. We don't want to repeat the cycle. We want it to end with us so that our kids will have an easier time raising their kids.

To break this cycle, we must learn to pause, take a deep breath and be still. Pausing allows us the necessary time to disengage our reptilian brain and engage our thinking brain. We must pause and think, 'If I react this way, how will I be affecting my child?" without knowing it, we are modeling proper anger management to our kids.

Big emotions are a message that something is not working in our lives. But emotions such as anger do not help us find the best solution to the problem, and that is why anger makes us say and do things we did not mean. The fight-flight mode makes the other person the enemy, and we either want to fight them or flee from them.

When you identify a pain point, you need to reset the meaning of the story. Everyone went through challenging times as children, and it is impossible to go back. What we can re-write is the meaning we took that formed a belief. If your mother left when you were little and never came back, it is time to understand that you had nothing to do with it and nothing you could have done as a child would have brought her back.

The advantage we have now as we look back and reflect at situations that made us angry, anxious or doubt ourselves is that we have grown up. Thus, we have more information now than we did then. We are more rational, and we look at the situation as an adult would. It may take some time to rewrite these painful moments and fully accept the truth we present now, but it is liberating and the only way to not inflict the same pain we experienced on our kids.

Being a parent is hard work and is tougher when you are stressed. Developing a de-stressing system or routine will help us release some of the stress and give us the peace we need to discipline and not punish. After a long day at work, it is easy to take out the stressful meetings we had on our little ones without our knowledge.

Coffee with a friend, cardio workout, meditation, jogging, yoga, or spa treatment will help lower our stress to manageable levels or bring us back to equilibrium. Setting time apart to direct all our aggression on a treadmill instead of our kids may not always be possible. But there are other ways to do it. Put the kids to bed early and have a quiet time where nobody is asking you questions or expecting anything from you, or catch up on some sleep. Blast some music and dance with your kids without a care in the world who will see you. Take a step back and slow down. Sometimes, you don't have to be in a hurry as such.

Sometimes, working through the old is overwhelming, and it may weigh you down. Even as parents we need support and an opportunity to talk about the hard work we are doing, our fears and anxieties and not to be judged for feeling the way we do. There is no shame in needing a support system, reach out, it helps.

Connecting vs. Spoiling

When parents heal their painful pasts, and they are de-stressed, connecting with children becomes easy. Parents always wonder if all this positive parenting will spoil their kids and they end up with little brats? It is essential to identify what spoiling is and what it is not.

Spoiling has nothing to do with the time, attention and love you give your child. It has nothing to do with respect, independence and right decision making. An infant is not spoilt because you hold them and meet their needs when they cry. Responding to and soothing a child, nurturing your relationship with your child will not spoil them.

Spoiling occurs when a child is raised to feel that they must get their way whether that involves disregarding other people's needs or not. A spoilt child will expect their needs to be met instantly. She will expect everything to be done for her when she needs it and how she wants it. That's not what we are advocating for here. We want our kids to expect that their needs will be met, but we do not want them to assume their desires and whims met all the time. They will get what they need even when children don't understand what they want. Connecting with your child is about giving them what they need, not what they want.

Spoiling occurs when we praise our kids all the time and overindulge them by giving them too much stuff, spend too much money on them, and saying 'yes' all the time. It occurs when we give our children the notion that people will serve their whims.

Parents confuse indulge and connection. When we give children what they want all the time, we deny them the opportunity to learn resilience and deny them the joy of knowing that they have to work for what they want. Things are not just given; you work for them. We deny them an opportunity to learn how to deal with disappointments, yet the world is bound to disappoint them many times over and over again. They become entitled instead of grateful and will be ill-prepared to deal with life when things don't turn out the way they wanted.

When playing in the park, your son throws a fit because he is jealous of a toy another child is playing with. Asking the other child's mother if your son can have the toy so he would calm down is spoiling him. You deny him a chance to learn how to work out his anger and jealousy.

When your little girl cries her heart out in the grocery store for a sweet that gives her tonsils, and you buy it anyway, you are spoiling her. She learns that as long as she throws a tantrum, her needs will be met, even when they put her health at risk.

When you call a parent to ask if your son can get invited to a party he heard about but was not invited to, you are spoiling him and denying him a chance to learn how to deal with disappointment.

Connecting is walking through the hard times with your child and being there for them when they cannot control their emotions or behavior. We are building independence by understanding our child's emotional control struggle and guiding them through it instead of reprimanding them for losing control. When they feel safe and connected, their neurons wire in a way that builds emotional and rational skills to face what life brings their way head-on.

When your child has an outburst and hits her sister because she would not share a toy, hugging her and helping her take a breath to calm down is connecting.

When your son throws his truck towards a jar, hopefully, missed it, because he is angry and you say "I understand you are upset and having a hard time controlling your anger because you can't take your truck to school" is connecting.

Refusing to give your child ice-cream on a cold morning and allowing her to cry it out as you hold her is connecting.

How to connect with your child

Parents are human, and with the busy life we live today, it is easier to meet the most basic needs of a child without putting effort to meet emotional needs. To help us connect with them at a deeper level, we need to be deliberate about it. As a parent, you can:

- Have routines that reconnect you with your child during the day like snuggles in the morning or after an afternoon nap.
- Give an emotional refuel before you separate with your child. Hugs and kisses before you leave for work, during bedtime, and before you drop them to school.
- Physical touch such a simple hug. Hug them in the morning when they wake up and in the evening before bed, hug them before you go to work and when you come back just because hugs are awesome and help us connect.
- Do not interact with technology when you have special time with your child. She will know that she is so important that you put aside your phone to listen to her.
- Have family time almost every day if not every day. Dinner time can be reserved for the family. Stop working before dinner time so that you can play and connect with your kids. Switch off your phones and the television during dinner to avoid distractions so that your family can have your full attention.
- Spare special time for your child. Spend time with each child individually from time to time. Play a game, go out for ice cream, make your child laugh, or dance and sing.

- Connect to their level and adjust to your child's emotions. It is impossible for children to come up to your level, so go down to their level and connect from their state.
- Do not withdraw, even when your child drives you away. Without nagging or pestering them, let them know you are there for them and you will help them work out their emotions when they are ready.

Set clear firm limits in a loving and respectful way

Setting boundaries without hurting our children can be a task. We would rather dish out commands on what they need to do and how they should get it done. It's so much easier.

"Don't hit your sister."

"Fasten your seatbelt."

Sometimes kids feel justified even when they have done something wrong. For parents who are transitioning from spanking to positive parenting, setting limits without punishing your kids when they misbehave, especially hitting other kids poses a challenge.

When they do something wrong, they are spanked; that is the model they know. So, when someone does something they feel is wrong; naturally, they will punish them.

John was playing with his toy once when he suddenly started hitting it. "I said it's time to sleep. I should not repeat myself." This may be the exact words, or something close to what his mother uses when scolding him. John felt the need to spank his toy because it was not cooperating with his bedtime.

Ivy and Nina were playing with dolls when Ivy hit her sister.

"Nina it hurts when you hit someone. Please don't hit your sister" may be answered by "Why can't I hit her, but you get to hit me?".

"I know you feel bad your sister does not want to share. But hitting hurts, that's why I don't do it anymore, and I am sorry I used to hit you. It hurts when you hit someone; please don't hit your sister."

What you have done is that you have admitted your mistake, which made you connect with your child and set the boundary on hitting other people by repeating that they should not beat their sister. A strong-willed child will continue to argue, and it will take you real effort to remain calm.

This does not mean that you should allow your child to behave the way they want, just because they cannot control themselves, that would be irresponsible. A visit to the toy store is both enjoyable and challenging. Imagine your child throws a tantrum because you won't buy him a toy you feel is too advanced for him.

Telling your child that they seem upset would not help the situation. This will allow him to hold everyone captive, which is not fair for the other parents shopping for toys. It also empowers your child to continue throwing a tantrum, hoping that you will give in to the demand.

"I can see that you are disappointed that you will not be getting that toy. I can help you if you let me. You are now connecting to your child's emotions (disappointment) and offer help, allowing your child to calm himself while reassuring him that you are there for him. Does this mean you get him the toy? No, if the answer was no before the tantrum, it should be no after the outburst.

This way your son learns that there is a limit to what he is allowed to do, touch, engage with and behave like. He also determines that there are no compromises just because he has thrown a tantrum or is disappointed with something. Connecting with kids emotionally makes it possible for us to help them make good choices and respect boundaries.

Children instincts are not to hold everyone else, hostage, because they feel out of control. We can teach them that relationships flourish with respect, consideration, cooperation, and compromise. Please pay attention to their internal world while holding on to the standards will see children learn connection and respect boundaries.

Good children and bad behavior
In the 1950s, children were thought to be inherently evil and harsh punishments were used to correcting their bad behavior. With time, parents realized that there is no bad kid, just bad behavior. This statement is the foundation of positive parenting. Children are learning limits and how they should behave. Their bad behavior is an experiment and an opportunity to determine what is acceptable.

When playing with other kids at the park and your son hits another child, you feel embarrassed and fear that your child may be a mean person. Notice that a child will also feel bad when they hit another child, and they cry. The pain the other child feels is mirrored, and they feel sorry for their action. Although they do not understand motives well, they already think that maybe hitting the other boy was not a good idea and your child is already regretting it (though he can't accurately pinpoint what they are feeling).

Calling your child, a bad boy or bad girl reinforces the negative feelings and form a negative image of your child in your mind and your child's mind. You might have heard a parent say "my son is very aggressive and hits people a lot; that's just the way he is." This parent has accepted that their son is 'bad' and is likely to reinforce the same feelings in her son.

However, your son may be experiencing a stress trigger that made him act out. Maybe he was angry the other boy took his toy or said something means to him. His environment must have contributed to his outburst causing him to misbehave. Accepting that the behavior was bad, but the child is good, makes positive parenting easier.

Finding out why your son hit another child will make him feel accepted and heard, then tell him the acceptable behavior he should have shown.

"I understand that you felt angry he took your toy. Instead of hitting our friends, we ask them politely to return our toy."

It would be nice if your child replied with "Yes mom, I understand. I promise to use my words next time and restrain myself from harming other kids," but this is not likely. If your child is already feeling guilty about what they did, they are likely to start crying. If they are still angry, they will talk back.

Please do not lose your calm, continue to engage your child's thinking brain until they are entirely calm and understand the lesson. If they cry, hug them to make them feel safe and accepted at their most vulnerable time. Whichever the reaction you get, in your mind and your child's, you have planted a seed that it was bad behavior, not a bad child.

Give guidance and offer choices

Children like to feel that they are in control of their lives. They don't want to be given commands all the time. By giving them choices, we empower our kids and show them that we trust them to make decisions.

When going out for a walk, you want your child to be in comfortable shoes and clothes. Asking her to choose which pair of sneakers she wants to wear and whether she prefers to walk in tights or shorts will reduce the hustle. If she picks out what she wants to wear, she will wear it quickly or cooperate as you help her.

A word of caution though. Be sure that you are comfortable with the choices you give. Giving a child an option, you cannot abide with makes you unreliable in their eyes. If you become fond of this, your child will soon start answering you with "I don't know or just choose for me" which shows that they feel that even if they say what they want, you will shoot it down and make your own choice anyway, so why bother?

Parents can start by giving choices that are not too complicated like what shoes to wear. Some decisions like what to cook for dinner may be too complicated for toddlers. The likelihood of choosing a healthy meal is slim, and frankly, they will probably want to eat out than wait for you to cook boring broccoli. A great trick to use is to give them two options to choose from especially when you will be preparing a meal they like. When you do decide to eat out, asking her to pick her lunch or the restaurant to eat at will automatically work.

Adele Feber and Elain Mazlish in their book "How to talk so kids will listen and listen, so kids will talk" stated that giving children choices fosters independence and autonomy. Each decision they make gives them control over their life. Children are entirely dependent on us, but when a person is wholly dependent on another, feelings of helplessness, unworthiness, frustration, anger, and resentment emerge. To reduce a child's bitterness, we should offer them a choice about how something is done.

"I can see you dislike this medicine. Would it be easier to take it with some juice?

Choices give our children the needed practice in decision making. As adults, they will be expected to choose their career, a mate, where to live, their lifestyle and how to tackle problems at their workplace without our help. Through the choices we expose them to, they are likely to feel more confident about themselves and the choices they make in the future.

When you respect your child's choice, he is likely to struggle to see it through and ask for help when he hits a dead end. However, giving an option is not always easy. The sheer convenience of doing everything to save time or get it over and done will tempts parents, all the time.

We live in a busy world that requires us to move at high speeds all the time. It's just easier to wake our kids, choose what to wear and dress them, tell them what to eat and always remind them to hurry up or they will be late.

But protecting our children so much takes away their hopes, dreams, and aspirations and may hinder them from achieving their goals. Choices let them know that they are not entirely helpless, but separate, responsible, competent people.

Another challenge we face as parents are; allowing our children to fail and feel disappointed when we would have told them what to do. We think that their failure is our own and we give in to the temptation of moving in and helping before they ask for our help.

"What should I do?" your elementary schooler asks when she shares a problem she is having with her friends.

"What do you think you should do?" would be an excellent place to start. As they figure out the solution to the problem, sit still and listen. It is tempting to interject when they go with something entirely off but don't.

By asking "how will he feel about that" will remind them to look at the situation from their friends' point of view and consider his feelings. Your daughter will then go back to looking for options.

Bribes vs. Praise and Encouragement
As a parent, you will have the most impact on your child's development, both physically and emotionally. Your child's mental health will depend on how you raise them which makes it crucial for you to do your best when he is growing up.

Praising a child is like using a double-edged sword. Praise has some inbuilt problems of its own. It can make you doubt yourself. For example, let us assume your child comes back from school with a drawing. She did not put much effort into drawing it but just scribbled something because she was bored. When going through her book, you notice the picture and say "wow, this is a good drawing

Joanna." Remembering what little effort she put in it, Joanna immediately doubts herself, probably thinking that you are either lying, or you don't know what a good drawing looks like.

Praise can also lead to anxiety. Let's assume that your child cannot color coordinate and will put on clothes in the weirdest color combination. Today, however, he walks into the kitchen with a white shirt and blue jeans. You are impressed that he did not pick a red shirt with green pants again. "Good job on the color coordination" you affirm. John sulks and thinks how bad he will feel next time he does not coordinate colors right.

Praise can make your child doubt themselves, can be threatening and make them focus on their weaknesses instead of their strength. It can also come out as manipulative where your child wonders what you want from them. Paul Donahue, Ph.D. says that constant praise poses a risk of putting your child on a pedestal. The child feels pressured to get your approval all the time and continuously look for validation.

When praise is sincere and focused on the effort, not the outcome, giving it as often as possible will not harm your child. The approval is in the effort, not the finished product. When a good habit has already been engraved in your child, you do not need to keep praising him for it, instead, praise him when he does something out of the ordinary, especially where the real effort has been used.

When he gets on a new ride in the amusement park, you can mention in passing how brave he is, but don't overdo it since he is not working hard but having fun. When he practices shooting hoops every day, runs drills and makes a few more baskets today than he did yesterday, praise him, he worked hard for it.

Experts agree that cash should not be used to praise or reward behavior. If we say to our kids "I will give you $5 if you get an A in geometry," we are teaching them to be motivated by money rather than positive feelings on success. Instead, we should use this as opportunities to celebrate their hard work and achievement. We can take them out for ice cream or special meals after a good game or good report card, which would encourage persistence and hard work.

When giving praise, statements such as 'what a beautiful drawing,' 'good job,' 'that's brilliant' and 'way to go' are neither specific nor evoke the encouragement we want our kids to feel. The more extravagant the praise we offer, the more our kids are likely to reject it as not genuine. People, not just children, perceive words that evaluate (good, beautiful, fantastic, brilliant) as uncomfortable.

According to Adel Feber and Elaine Mazlish, praise comes in two parts. The first part involves using a description with an appreciation for what you see while the second part consists of the child praising himself after hearing the description.

"You cleaned your room? What a good girl you are" becomes "I can see much work has been going on here. All the clothes are in the closet, the blocks are back on the shelves, and every marble has been picked up".

When you describe your enthusiasm, your children learn to appreciate their strengths. It will take a lot more effort to use description when praising than it does to say great or excellent. The more you do it, the easier it becomes second nature.

According to Feber and Mazlish, you can add to the description one or two words that sum up the child's good behavior, telling the child something about himself and the skill he is developing. For instance, your child loves cake, but they only ate one piece.

"You only ate a little slice of cake even though you like it, that takes willpower." Here, your child learns that you appreciate that they did not stuff themselves with cake and they discover that they are developing willpower.

The good boy is quickly taken away by a bad boy, but a thoughtful description of the card he made his mother when she was sick will never be taken away, it is stored in his emotional bank. This memory becomes the go-to emotion when his teacher asks who wants to make a goodbye card for the kid transferring to another school in a different state. It becomes his go-to place when he is faced with a creative project at work when he is an adult.

Because we are teaching children how to behave, parents tend to be quick to point out what a child did wrong and slow to praise. But when you look at the world, it is as swift to offer criticism as we are. Being different at home is the best place for our kids to learn to assert themselves and affirm their rightness.

Self-esteem is built on real accomplishment. It drives from knowing that we have what it takes to share our gifts with the world and make out dreams a reality. Self-esteem is not a one-time feeling. It is an acquired state that comes through repetition and becomes a way of life. It is easy to assume that some children are more goal-oriented, talented and self-motivated than others but this is a result, not a cause.

All children are born with talents and the more they learn how to enjoy the creative process of making things happen, whether they succeed or fail, the more their resilience and self-esteem is built. Some children find it more challenging to learn how to read, remember their backpacks and build relationships. Supporting this child in areas, they need help and praising them when they do well build up their esteem and gives them the confidence they need to keep trying every time they fall.

Sometimes, our parenting skills fail us and the only way to act at the moment is to bribe our way out of the situation. While most parents use this from time to time to get out of a problematic situation, experts advise that we are teaching children to get rewards for behavior they should have.

Laura Markham, Ph.D. says that all of us, including children, need an incentive from time to time to give up something we want. Just because we want our kids to obey us the moment we want them to do something does not mean they will. We are likely to do something when we know there is a reward in it for us, and for our kids, this could be an ice cream treat after leaving the park.

To make this work, Markham says that we need to look for a win-win situation where we reward in advance and not in the middle of misbehavior. Rewarding in the middle of misconduct teaches children to misbehave, so they get a reward.

Parents should, however, use incentives with caution. When children are rewarded for the desired behavior, we communicate that the behavior is unpleasant since you have to be rewarded for doing it. Whether you praise them for doing something they did not want to do or reward them, kids will only cooperate when you are watching, if you use this model of discipline.

Reading can be enjoyable, and a shower is refreshing, broccoli can taste good. Instead of manipulating with a bribe, it is best to use other positive discipline methods like pointing out the result of the behavior. "That is an exciting story. Or "Julie was pleased when you shared your doll with her."

While using incentives is not entirely discouraged, using them as a way out all the time to avoid challenging behavior is not encouraged. Children learn faster than adults do and giving them rewards to good behavior all the time trains them to do what we want so they get something.

When your five-year-old asks you what's in it for her or negotiates with you for a reward, so she does what you want, you have taken the reward too far. Your child still holds all the feelings that are causing her to misbehave inside her. While a reward is a good distraction, be ready to connect with her later and work out the feeling. This means that an incentive can only be used during an 'emergency.' A dinner party at your friend's place may be an emergency, but a store visit is not because she will soon be using tantrums to extort bribes every time you visit the store.

Teach emotions
Children are born with emotional reactions like crying, hunger, pain, and frustration and learn about key emotions from emotional, social and cultural context. During birth, children have eight primary emotions wired into their brains. These are fear, joy, anger, sadness, surprise, disgust, interest and shame. They express these emotions in different variations such as anxiety which is a form of fear and resentment a form of anger.

Secondary emotions (anxiety and resentment) stem from the eight primary emotions and are used to reflect emotional reactions to specific feelings. A child who is punished because she threw a fit may feel anxious to express her anger or jealousy the next time she gets triggers.

Our reaction to our children's emotions determines their emotional intelligence. As discussed in an earlier chapter, kids will behave better when they learn how to express their emotions. But how exactly can we help them express these emotions?

By giving them a framework that helps explain their emotions. This framework helps kids tame their emotions and use their logical mind to solve problems. It's hard to teach kids about their emotions because emotions are an abstract idea, difficult to explain. Sadness, fear, and excitement are hard to explain unless we use 'emotion teaching aids' to help kids identify them.

Emotions affect every choice a child makes. A child who can understand and identify their emotions finds it less likely to have a meltdown. If they can name it, they can tame it. If your child tells you that he is mad at you, he is less likely to hit you when you do not pay attention to his needs immediately. A child who can say "it hurt my feelings when…" is likely to resolve conflict peacefully.

Teach empathy
To effectively teach our kids how to handle their emotions and behavior, we must teach them empathy, the foundation of emotions. Daniel Gottam says that compassion is the foundation of positive parenting. Compassion gives you the essential backbone to understanding your child and preventing you from using 'past issues kaleidoscope' to discipline your children. Without

empathy, children will not feel loved, no matter how much we love them.

Empathy does not only comprise of viewing situations from the other person's point of view. It is also a physical event controlled by the right side of our brain which also controls intimacy and love. When our stomach leaps, our skin crawls or our heart skips a beat, the insula (connects the heart, the brain, and the digestive system) sends us a message. We feel it in our bodies. A more accurate definition of empathy is, therefore, feeling from the other person's point of view.

Empathy helps a child feel understood, less alone and the experience teaches her the most profound ways that humans connect. Children learn compassion naturally by experiencing empathy from their caregiver. Being empathetic to your child shows him that his emotions are not dangerous and shameful but universal and manageable.

Empathy does not call for permissiveness; setting limits is crucial. Acknowledge your child's unhappiness about the restrictions but maintain them nonetheless. It is essential to your child that you can tolerate his anger and disappointment towards you.

Empathy helps your child get over his upset feelings, and he can begin thinking about solutions by himself without you solving the problem for him. Listen and acknowledge without jumping in with a solution. Empathy will help you manage your anxiety about the issue and take a step back allowing your child to come up with a solution.

Empathy shows that although you understand his feelings, you don't necessarily endorse them. It is not questioning him and probing, but it is experiencing his situation without forcing him to share his feelings. Empathy is allowing him to feel the situation without invalidating his feeling.

Name emotions

Preschoolers can learn basic emotions. You can start with happy, sad, mad and scared. Older kids can understand more variants of these primary emotions. Happiness will include love, joy, and peace. Fear will consist of terror, anxiety, nervousness, and worry. Sadness will vary as grief, depression, and loneliness while anger will include frustration, bitterness, rage, and despair.

When your child is sad, asking her "do you feel a little sad that daddy left?" will make her aware of the emotion she is experiencing. To reinforce this, read a good book, and ask her what she thinks the character is feeling when she cries.

You can also comment on other people's emotions, as long as you do it in an accepting and nonjudgmental way at the park when the little girl hurts her knee and cries for her mother.

"That little girls hurt her knee. She must be in pain."

"Is there something special you can do to help her?"

During the day, create opportunities to talk about feelings by sharing your feelings. For example, you can tell him that you feel sad he does not want to play with his little brother or that his little brother is sad he does not want to play with him.

Use charts with different emotions that help your child identify them and name them. You can play a game where you make faces, and she tries to identify the emotions you may be feeling.

Learning and naming feelings is one thing; managing them is another thing altogether. Just because your child is angry does not mean they should hit their big brother, because she is sad does not mean she should take it out on you or other kids.

Whenever you are experiencing big emotions, primarily because of your child's misbehavior, model how they should deal with it, for instance, you can model how to pause and calm yourself when you are angry by taking a deep breath and remaining silent for a few minutes before you correct indiscipline.

When your child is calm, ask them to come up with ideas on how they can handle triggers that would set off their emotions. "You were disappointed that I would not play with you because I was working on a project. You were so disappointed that you became angry and hit me. When you feel angry and disappointed, what should you do?"

Praise your child when they handle themselves well. It takes effort for a child to say "I am mad at you because… or I am sad because…." When they first use their word to express how they are feeling, praise them. "I like how you told daddy you were sad. He had to apologize for not buying you the pair of school shoes." This will encourage your child to use her words more often than to throw a fit.

Feelings word chart

Brave	Cheerful	Confused
Curious	Proud	Bored

Disappointed	Frustrated	Embarrassed
Silly	Excited	Fantastic
Uncomfortable	Worried	Friendly
Stubborn	Generous	Shy
Satisfied	Ignored	Impatient
Relieved	Peaceful	Overwhelmed
Jealous	Interested	Loving
Lonely	Tensed	Angry
Calm	Afraid	Sorry
Mad	Joyful	Mean
Grumpy	Irritable	Alarmed
Awful	Bubbly	Calm
Tearful	Moody	Thankful
Sympathy	Pleased	Weird
Violent	Withdrawn	Heartbroken
Desperate	Relaxed	Miserable
Comfortable	Glad	Suspicious
Uneasy	Hopeful	Left out
Discouraged	Ashamed	Understood
Appreciated	Surprised	Confident

Choose your battles

Toddlers change a lot between 12 and 36 months. There is a massive change in their cognitive and language skills as well as their emotional development. Emotional outburst and unpredictable behavior are the order of the day. This emotional outburst can take a toll on parents, understandably because being triggered all the time puts us out of balance.

A lot of the things toddlers do is inconveniencing for parents and knowing when to choose a behavior to discipline, and one to ignore is not easy. Parents have been advised to ignore children during a tantrum to prevent them from behaving that same way in the future. However, we have established that tantrums are a result of unmet needs or big emotions that your child cannot control.

Ignoring children during their hour of need, in the name of preventing future tantrums, is taking us back to 1950 when children were thought to be manipulative, cunning, evil and inherently bad. While children can learn this undesired behavior and know when to push your buttons to get their way, children are intrinsically good, even when they misbehave.

It is interesting how a child's brain development works. It would fascinate parent's to know that children don't remember the last time they threw a fit. They don't remember the last time they climbed up they fell that is why they keep climbing up the ladder no matter how many times you ask them not to.

A child who tantrums and misbehaves is innocent, he is just expressing his unfulfilled needs, frustrations and is probably feeling powerless too. The more you connect with your child during this moment, the more you help them name their emotions, the less likely they are to a tantrum every time they are angry, sad or frustrated.

However, do all inconveniences that children cause need discipline? Let us consider some scenarios.

Scenario 1: It's after dinner, you usually read a book together once you finish doing the dishes. Your plastic items are places within your little ones reach. She picks them up, three at a go and head to the sitting room. She comes back for some more and soon; all the plastic cups are gone.

Scenario 2: You are reading a book as your little one is playing with blocks. On top of your book, you notice him laughing trying to get your attention as he pours the blocks from their holding container.

Scenario 3: You are busy making lunch. The house is awfully quiet so your toddler must be up to something, you go round only to find her perusing your magazines.

Scenario 4: You agree to help your child with a crossword puzzle before starting to prepare dinner.

When you are done, he insists on doing a second one.

If a child's needs are being fulfilled, but he continues to be annoying and troublesome, the wise thing would be to be firm and ignore them and let them work out their frustration by themselves. In scenario 4, the child's need to connect has been met, but he insists on more special time.

"I know you are disappointed. I can't help you with another crossword puzzle, but I have to start preparing dinner. The option I see is working on another one tomorrow or Sunday. You choose."

By giving your child an option, he knows that you are not ignoring his need to connect, but dinner needs to get started. Walking away teaches him delayed gratification, and he is likely to choose a time that is convenient for both of you.

A parent is not a policeman, acting like one can drain the energy of us and we find ourselves needing recharge more often than we should. Parents need a break and kids will be kids. They will touch things you don't want them to play with to get a little attention.

So, when your toddler plays with your magazines, or rearranges plastic cups, ignoring them would be more appropriate than disciplining them. You can lock the cupboard later and put the magazines where she can't reach them. This principle should only be used when the child is not likely to harm themselves. If she decides to rearrange glass utensils, you need to stop her before she breaks something and hurts herself.

Sometimes, children seek negative attention. Ignoring the misbehavior diminishes the fun of it and reduces the chance of future misconduct. So, if he pours his blocks for the sheer pleasure of it, then tries to get your attention, ignore him.

A parent should never ignore a child's needs, but ignoring purposeful negative behavior (as long as the child will not hurt themselves) can break you from being a policeman.

Redirect and be consistent

Stay calm, use your words, connect with your child, let them feel their emotions and know you are there for them. Okay! Got it!

When we read a book, attend a seminar or watch an online video on the positive effects our positive discipline habit will have on our kids, we get a lot of 'aha' moments and vow to live by the discoveries we have made until the rubber meets the road, and we lose it. We wonder, how does something that sounds so simple, like stay calm, name emotions, redirect and connect with our kids require such immense willpower and energy?

The truth is, no one can be 100% consistent in disciplining kids 100% of the time. When your three-year-old throws herself to the ground at the supermarket when half the store is watching, we are tempted to use punishment. However, consistency lets children know what to expect and how to make informed decisions. When they notice our inconsistency, they will keep pocking us, hoping to get a favorable outcome.

She cries for a toy today, and you buy it because you don't have the energy to deal with her tantrum, you have enough stress of your own. You will deal with her later.

The next time you go to the store, she throws a fit for a lollipop, you stand your ground and connect with her, she feels disappointed, but she opts for the healthier apple you offer.

When you take her with you for shopping next week, she is likely to throw a tantrum and demand for something else. Not because she cannot ask nicely, but because she is not sure of the outcome. It's like gambling.

You place a bet and pull the lever, then wait for the machine to give you the results. You are not sure if you will get sevens, cherries or lemons, but if you are lucky, you will hit the jackpot. This uncertainty is exactly what kids are experiencing with our inconsistency. When she throws a fit, she may get an outright no and be reprimanded with consequence and threats. There is also a possibility that she will get something even though it's not what they wanted, but if she is lucky, she will hit the jackpot and get precisely what they wanted.

Behavioral psychologists call this 'variable interval reinforcement schedule.' It is the most powerful type of reward system. For gamblers, the size of the reward keeps varying making it challenging to stop gambling. This reward system works the same way with our kids and makes it hard for them to stop playing the slot machine, which in this case is us, parents.

Children are growing beings. As kids become older, our inconsistency is likely to be viewed as a lack of authority. When children get no meaning behind why they should not behave in a certain way, the discipline you are fighting to instill loses meaning. Kids end up being confused and lack the necessary foundation they need to make sound decisions. Today they are here, tomorrow there and back to where they started. It's confusing and creates insecurity.

Parenting is hard work, and there is no refuting that. Coupled with the messy and chaotic world we live in, we are bound to make mistakes from time to time. We will forge things, confuse dates and sometimes we don't have the energy to deal with our kids' behavior. How can we keep it consistent without losing it?

Choose one behavior at a time

When trying new parenting techniques, choose one behavior to start with. Biting more than you can chew will get you confused, frustrated and worn out. An emotional crush when you cannot keep it together will do no good to your discipline efforts. Choose what you would see as a high priority issue like anger management, bedtime or stealing, and start with that.

The more you practice connecting with your child as you set limits in that area, the easier it becomes in other areas. You will have the advantages of the snowball effect. The more your child learns to control and name their anger, the less likely they are to hit others, call them names and throw a fit.

Foster routines

Keep the same schedule every day, as consistently as possible. Have regular nap times, meal times, fun times and bedtime, so that your child knows what is expected of them. This schedule will reduce the meltdown and make it easier for him to follow the plan.

If you need to change the schedule to include something different, like a birthday party, playdate or mom's visitor, inform him in advance. An alarm prepares him for a slight acceptable change and may avert a meltdown.

After lunch, a mom bathed her daughter and dressed her up in 'nice clothes.' The confused little girl kept asking her mother what was happening, but her mother would not disclose because she wanted to surprise her daughter with an afternoon visit to her grandmothers'.

When she finally learned that they were visiting grandma, the little girl started crying uncontrollably, not because she did not want to see her grandmother but because she felt that her feelings had were disregarded. She was looking forward to spending time with her mother playing games but now she wouldn't.

A big chance, like moving to a new city or the birth of a baby, needs to be handled with more care than a simple addition to the afternoon schedule. The dynamic of having a newborn baby taking all her parents' attention is complex for kids to understand as are the dynamics of moving and leaving all her friends behind. Preparing your child for the significant change that is coming her way will take some time.

Inform them a few months before the change to give them enough time to ask questions and gather information on what is about to happen to them. The more questions and information they seek the better. By the time you pack your bags to leave, or her little brother arrives, she will be comfortable and prepared to face the challenge that comes with a significant change.

Divert and re-direct

Diversion offers an advantage when disciplining our kids. Toddlers have a short concentration span that you can take advantage of and distract them from whatever they are worried about.

Let's take the little one who has a meltdown about going to grandma's place. Her routine dictated that she spends an hour playing with her mother and she feels threatened that this time is being taken away. To calm her down, her mother can distract her by picking one of her favorite board games.

Mom: "Look, Angie, I found your favorite game?" Once her attention is on you, you can continue with "why don't you carry it to grandma's place so we can play it there? It will be so much fun."

Little girl: "we don't have enough tiles. We are missing some."

Mom: Oh yeah! What do you think we should do?

Little girl: We can buy some at the supermarket

Mom: I am sure we can. Come on let's go.

Diversion is not only for kids. Parents need it as much as kids do. When you are feeling overwhelmed with all the parenting you have done for the day, taking a walk or a long bath will help you settle anxieties and recharge your parenting batteries.

Redirect

Children do not understand, 'no,' the same way adults do. According to Dr. Jane Nelson, 'no" is an abstract concept that is counterproductive to a child's development needs to explore their world and develop a sense of autonomy and initiative.

Your child may know you do not want him to do something and you will get angry at him if he does it, but he does it anyway because he cannot understand why he shouldn't. His version of knowing something lacks the internal control necessary to stop him.

According to research by Jean Piaget, children do not understand cause and effect making it a challenge for them to understand consequences and ethics. These higher order thinking may not develop until the child is age 10.

To illustrate, take two same sizes playing dough and ask your toddler if they are the same and if one is bigger or small. When he agrees that they are the same, take one playing dough and smash it with your hands, then put it down again. Ask your toddler if they are the same. He will say they are not and will tell you that the smashed one is smaller.

This experiment illustrates that our interpretation of an event will be very different from our child's analysis of the same event. At the age of one, your child is at the 'I do it' stage where she develops a sense of autonomy vs. doubt and shame. At age two through six, she develops initiative vs. guilt where she explores and experiments.

It must be very confusing then for a child when they get punished for developing. She wonders if she should follow her autonomy and initiative in exploring the world or follow her parent's rules. Just because they are growing does not mean we should let children do whatever they want, which is where supervision, distraction, and redirection comes in.

We must show them what to do instead of telling them what they should not do.

"When you hit your brother because he ignored you, it hurts. Why don't you tap them instead? Here let me show you how it's done."

For toddler and preschoolers, supervision, kindness, and firmness are an essential tool in disciplining. When your toddler wonders off into the kitchen and comes back holding a knife, spanking and reprimanding him will get the immediate effect of putting the knife down. Will spanking stop the toddler from picking up a knife next time he sees one? Probably not.

Kindly and firmly, direct the young one to more acceptable objects, like his toys and continue to do so until the message sinks in.

Redirecting ideas for parents
- Don't lecture

As parents, we often feel the need to lecture our children and point out what they did wrong and explain in detail what needs to happen next time. We might even repeat it a couple of times or ask them to repeat it to make sure the message is home. The last thing anyone wants, including children, is a lecture about their mistake and pop up quiz after the lecture. The parent will often ask their kids "Are you even listening to me?" during these lectures because all the child is hearing is "Good behavior blah blah blah blah." We must address the behavior obviously, but as we do, we keep it short and precise. Even toddlers don't like lectures and to make matters worse they have no brain capacity to internalize everything you are saying.

Once you address the child's behavior, redirect. By moving on immediately, we avoid giving negative emotions too much energy and instead get back on track. If you need to cover an issue extensively, ask questions and listen to the answer. A collaborative discussion will lead to a better understanding of the behavior and the emotions behind the behavior.

- Address emotions

Kids are sometimes unable to distinguish between their emotions and actions. During redirecting, let your child understand that their emotions are normal. There is nothing wrong with feeling so frustrated that you want to destroy something, but saying it's okay to 'feel like it' doesn't mean you should do it. This distinction shows children that it's what they do after their emotions that determine if their behavior is acceptable or not.

"I understand you are angry at your sister, but snatching her doll and throwing it on the ground isn't how we treat each other. Let's talk about other ways to express your anger."

When we undermine our children's feelings, kids begin to doubt their ability to observe and comprehend what's going on within them, which will leave them confused and disconnected to their emotions. We want them to believe that as they learn about right and wrong behavior, their feelings and experiences will be honored, respected and validated. The number of disciplinary actions will continue to reduce.

- Use descriptions

Going back to what Piaget observed, we have established that kids do not see situations from our perspective. The best way to bring them up to our level is to describe what we are seeing, and our kids will get what we are saying.

"Uh! Throwing the blocks makes it hard to build" would make sense to a toddler while "I still see clothes on the floor" would be easily understood by an older child. Such statements open a door for dialogue and learning than an immediate reprimand. "Do we talk to people like that?"

More often than not, all parents need to do is pay attention to the behavior they are seeing. Children already know how to distinguish right from wrong in most situations. By drawing attention to the behavior, they are reminded of the limits you have set and the expected behavior.

"Looks like Anna wants to color the nose" is not fundamentally different from "Let your sister color the nose" but the former offers advantages over the latter. Your child will not be put into a defensive mode which will awaken his reptilian mind, shutting down his thinking mind. It also allows him to exercise his thinking mind and develop an internal compass.

"Anna is feeling left out sitting all by herself" gives her a chance to observe the situation and determine what needs to happen. This shows our child that we are ready to hear an explanation and gain some insight before we draw any conclusions on the matter. We also allow her to defend herself without engaging her reptilian brain or going into the fight-flight mode.

- Get the child involved

Communication in a disciplinary moment has always included the parent lecturing (talking) and the child ignoring (listening). Discipline becomes much more effective when we initiate a dialogue instead of giving a monologue. With dialogue, we do not forego our authority figures in the relationship.

Let's say your daughter is angry at her little brother and she snatched his truck and throws it across the room breaking it. Once you calm the little boy and connect with your daughter you say something like "Liz, I know that you are mad at your brother and that's ok. Everyone gets mad sometimes. However, when you get angry, you need to control the actions. Throwing other people's things only makes them sad and escalates the situation. Next time you need an appropriate way to express your feelings."

While there is nothing wrong with this statement, the approach is offering a monologue where the mother corrects the behavior, and the child receives the information. What if you involve her in a dialogue?

Mom: You were mad at your brother a while back that you threw his track. What was going on? (connect, respect, understand her feelings)

Liz: I was just furious (feels validated, respected and heard)

Mom: Then you threw his track? (brings attention to the behavior.)

Liz: Sorry, I shouldn't have thrown his truck. (remembers the lesson you have taught her)

Mom: There is nothing wrong with getting angry; we sometimes do. How could you handle it next time? (invite problem-solving)

Initiating a discussion about an issue, especially when your kids know you are cutting back will get your kids invested in the conversation to ensure their interests (read: limits you set) are looked into. Although you will be the final decision maker, children learn that their input is valuable, they are respected, and you trust their problem-solving skills. There are times when you do not have room for discussion, times to allow your child to deal with disappointment, but dialogue ends in a win-win solution.

- Use conditional yes

When there is no wiggle room in a discussion, how you say 'no' matters. A straight 'no' is harder to accept than a yes with conditions. A straight no, especially if spoken harshly will immediately connect to the reptilian brain prompting the child to fight, flee, freeze or in extreme cases, faint. A supportive yes, even when it does not permit a behavior, opens the child to receiving and makes learning easier.

To a toddler who enjoyed the zoo so much, you can say "Of course we can stay a little longer in the zoo with the Lions next weekend when daddy drives us a little earlier to the zoo, but right now we have to leave." Your child will not be getting what they want right now, but at least they will come to the zoo earlier next weekend. Here, you are acknowledging the desire and building structure and skill (delayed gratification).

What would an alternative look like? "I know you want to stay because the zoo has all these great animals. Let's buy a teddy lion so you can play with him during the week before we visit the zoo next weekend."

Your child will learn to be proactive and sense the possibility of the future and create future actions in his imagination to meet your needs as a parent. Next time you leave the park, you might hear him say "I am sad we have to go now, but we will come back next weekend."

Here, you teach your child how to tolerate disappointment when things don't go as they would have hoped, but you are assisting them through their frustrations. Conditional yes will work with older children as well. "I have a lot on my plate right now, so yes let us paint a picture tomorrow when I have more time."

Please pay attention to your tone when denying a child something they want. It is crucial you don't appear arrogant, or the effect will be the same as that of an outright no. A conditional yes show your child that you care about their desire, even when they cannot be met immediately.

There are times we must just say no, but more often than not, we can find a way to give a conditional yes than deliberately turn away our kids. The things kids want for themselves are the very things we wish for.

- Be creative

There is nothing like one size fit all when it comes to parenting. Parents need to be flexible enough to pause and think of various responses and their implications to a situation, putting into consideration our parenting style and the child's temperament and development stage.

By exercising flexibility and creativity, we apply our thinking brain and easily conjure empathy, communication and the ability to disconnect our reactivity (reptilian brain). Humor is powerful to use with younger children. By using humor, you can change the dynamic of the interaction by talking in a silly voice or falling comically. Chasing mom to the car makes leaving the park more fun, especially if she screams and crackles in fear. Playfulness can crack a child's high emotions and calm her, so she gains control of herself.

It works with older children as well. Be ready for an eye roll or two or a sly remark here and there. The brain loves novelty and introducing it to something it has not seen before or expected; it will give its full attention. The minds first instinct is to determine if a situation is safe. When you introduce a new element, the mind goes to what is unique, new or different to identify if it's safe or not.

Humour also communicates the absence of threat which opens us up. Creative approaches come in handy when other forms of discipline are not working so well. If your elementary schooler has refused to do her homework on time, it's time to get creative.

Having a secret language or secret sign that only the two of you know about might make the homework more enjoyable. You can use the secret language to signal your child to start homework, and they signal you back when they need help and when they are done.

Creativity takes a lot more energy that we want to invest, and that's understandable. However, the flip side would be to use an unsuitable method that is not working which will wear you down faster and risk you going back to the default setting of punishment. The truth is, we can often avoid a battle or climbing a discipline hill when we become creative.

- Strengthen their mind

The bottom line is teaching children that they do not need to be stuck in negative experiences or be victims of external events or internal emotions. They can use their minds to take charge of how they feel and how they act. Helping children deal effectively with stressful situations increases their confidence in having a say in how they think and perceive the world.

Research indicates that if you provoke kids with the right mental tools that give them a strategy on how to handle experiences (especially delayed gratification), they are likely to manage their emotions, desires, and behavior better. These children also end up being more successful at school, relationship and as adults.

When children are facing difficult situations, we do not want them to deny that experience or try to suppress it. We want them to communicate and describe their inner experience, what they are seeing and feeling. We also want them to observe what is going on within them and how that impacts them. We want children to learn how to survey themselves and then problem solve based on awareness. Studying themselves allows them to own what is going on and not be stuck in a negative experience.

Chapter 7: Parenting styles and discipline

According to the American Psychological Association (APA), parenting practices share three common goals. The first is to ensure children are safe and healthy, the second to prepare children to become productive adults and the third to transmit cultural values.

Being a successful parent is not an easy job, but whether children become healthy, productive, competent adults depend on environmental and biological factors. There are a lot more influences that determine the outcome of a child. The parenting style you use is an integral part of the equation.

The particular parenting style you use may cause disruptive behavior such as attention deficit, hyperactivity disorders, and conduct problems. The parenting style used in psychology today is based on research by Diana Baumrind, a developmental psychologist. In her study, she noted that preschoolers exuded three types of behavior that were influenced by a specific type of parenting. She identified these parenting styles as authoritative, authoritarian and permissive parenting.

Maccoby and Martin expanded this model and used a two-dimensional framework to make further distinctions on Baumrind's permissive parenting style. This led to two different parenting styles, indulgent and neglectful parenting.

The four parenting styles are further grouped into two major categories: demandingness where parents control their child's behavior or demand maturity and responsiveness where parents are accepting and sensitive to their child's behavior and needs.

Authoritarian parent

An authoritarian parent has high expectations of their child and attempts to control, shape and evaluate a child's behavior and attitudes to align with set principals. Although wanting your child to fall in line is not entirely a bad thing, an authoritarian parent shows low responsiveness to their child's need and use commands and punishment to achieve discipline.

When a child questions why she cannot use food color to paint her sun yellow, an authoritarian parent will answer with a "because I said so" rather than giving a logical explanation. The child has no choice or opinion in any matter. The little one is expected to follow orders and commands without questioning or complaining failure to which punishment will follow.

This is the main parenting style used by parents in the 1950s. Although their mode of punishment was extreme than it is today, children in the 1950s had no rights to speak unless spoken to, were not allowed to share their opinion and had to control their emotions at all times. An authoritarian parent acts as a policeman, always looking for mistakes and ready to send their child to prison (time-out).

An authoritarian parent is also the judge and jury and will convict their child to whichever punishment they see fit. They attempt to control their child's behavior by monitoring their activity in and out of the home. This is the parent who wants to know every detail of where their child is at all times, who they are with and what they are doing.

They decide for their children, giving the child no room to figure out a solution to a problem by themselves. This parent does not consult with their child when making a decision that will affect the child, but they expect the child to accept the decision without complaining. They are rigid, restrictive, and punitive.

The effect this style of parenting and discipline has on children is enormously negative. Children raised in this parenting style learn to depend on their parents and are incapable of making their own decision. As adults, such children make decisions based on what their parents would do, rather than what is right.

Children in authoritarian homes are also timid, anxious and fearful. They have low self-esteem and will rarely volunteer in class or be comfortable handling a task by themselves. They follow instructions not because they understand them, but because they want to avoid punishment.

These children also learn that their emotions are dangerous and work hard to suppress them. They are likely to develop aggressive behavior because of the harsh treatment they received from their parents. They may also misbehave to protest against their parents, even when they know it's a losing battle and the consequences are dire.

The harsh treatment and punishment also cause children to feel unhappy and dissatisfied with their life. These parenting and discipline styles contribute significantly to the increase in depression and delinquency among children.

Permissive parent

Baumrind's research states that permissive parents are non-punitive, accepting and affirmative to their kid's behavior and needs. While these are positive aspects of parenting advocated in this book, permissive parents have one major weakness. They do not have set rules or principals that govern their kid's behavior.

They give their children full autonomy and encourage them to do what they want. Children learn to govern themselves from an early age, but without their parent's sound guidance. They are forgiving and use the philosophy of 'kids will be kids' to rear their kids.

They give privileges when their child begs and allows him to get out of time-out if he promises to be good. They are more of a friend to their child than a parent. While they encourage their children to share their problems, they rarely discourage their kids from making bad choices and never give guidance on how to make good choices.

The lack of involvement, consistency, and confidence in their parenting skills make it more difficult to correct their child's behavior and set firm, clear boundaries. These children are likely to be poor in decision making although they seem more mature and responsible than other kids.

Children raised by permissive parents are likely to fall into depression because their parents are too lenient, though they are supportive because they have no one to teach them how to focus and develop good judgment.

Permissive parents show less care for their kids, and they grow up alone without getting attention, develop low self-esteem, poor problem-solving skills, defiant to rules, no self-control, egotistic tendencies and have problems forming relationships and in social interactions.

Kids will prevent others from using toys and throw tantrums when they are defeated. They will even fight physically with other kids to get their way. Their children lack empathy and will laugh at another child when he cries, then feel confused when they see everyone else concern about the hurt child. Their kids may also have health problems because their parents do not limit junk food.

Neglectful parent

This parent shows low support and low control for their kids. These parents have little knowledge of what their children are doing and will not set firm boundaries and high standards. They set few rules and give no guidance, nurturing and parental attention to their children's needs.

A neglectful parent is not always intentional in their neglect. Some suffer from mental health issues such as maternal problems from physical abuse and neglect when they were kids, or suffer from substance abuse. Sometimes, they are overwhelmed with issues like bills, work and managing the household that they find it too exhausting to deal with their kids.

Children receive basic needs but will never have their emotional needs met. The parent is undemanding, insensitive and disconnected to her kids.

Kids suffer from low self-esteem and experience low satisfaction in life compared to their peers. They are likely to fall into depression compared to kids raise from authoritative, authoritarian and permissive homes. The kids are sad and confused about what they should do, how they should behave and often feel helpless.

Kids are anti-social and aggressive and will enter into fights more often. According to research, aggression and antisocial behavior in the United States has been attributed to parents neglecting their children. In 2005, a study by the US

Department of Health and Human Service concluded that the majority of parents in the United States use this parenting style which is the least desirable parenting style.

Neglectful behavior encourages delinquent behavior such as stealing, school difficulties and may lead to criminal behavior in adulthood. The children are disrespectful, violent and immoral. They, however, have good relationships with friends because they spend most of their time with them. They feel unloved by their parents and are resentful.

Authoritative parent

This is the most desirable parenting style. Parents who use this model show high responsiveness and set high standards for their children. They set rules and let children experience consequences naturally. When setting rules, parents put into consideration their children's opinion, making them feel heard and included in decision making. This teaches children to trust their problem-solving and decision-making skills.

Parents validate their children's feelings and help them manage their emotions when they lose control. Children are taught how to use tools and strategies to calm themselves and engage their thinking brain when emotions run high. They learn that just because you are experiencing an emotion does not mean you should act on it. When emotions are high, there is no reason and to engage reason, you must tactfully set emotions aside.

Authoritative parents invest a lot of time and energy in rearing their kids. They offer guidance and look for preventive measures to bad behavior in their kids. They are prone to using positive discipline to reinforce good behavior and encourage it to be repeated in the future.

As a result, their children are happy and successful. They're confident and can express their opinion without holding back while putting into consideration the other person's feelings. They are creative in problem-solving and perform better in school. Their parents help them to build social competences that leads to strong bonds with their peers and good relationships.

Children are likely to own their actions and make amends when they error. They are also expected to look for strategies to prevent the misbehavior in future creatively. They have a sense of responsibility and will be first to help another child when they fall into trouble. They are independent and have a high resilience developed from delayed gratification.

The exception
Sometimes parents do not fit into one category so don't be worried if there are times you are permissive, neglectful or authoritarian. While authoritative is the most desired parenting style, there have been some exceptions.

For instance, some kids may have authoritative parents but still perform poorly in school if they are still unable to form relationships with other kids. Human beings have a deep desire to connect with others, and when this connection lacks in school, where kids spend more of their time, kids end up being lonely and feel unloved. They may even doubt themselves and question their ability as they try to figure out why 'nobody likes them.'

Some kids, on the other hand, perform best when they have authoritarian parents and peer support. The high expectations their parents set for them academically, coupled with good relationships form a thriving foundation for their academic excellence.

A child's temperament also impacts the parenting style. A sensitive child is perceived more difficult which tempts many parents to be authoritarian, while this is not always the best model; parents may feel like their hand is forced.

Conflicting parenting styles and their effect on discipline

At some point, parents are not going to agree on how best to parent their kids. Dad may feel that mom is too strict while mom may feel that dad is too lenient. Parenting styles started evolving in each one of us where we were little children. How we were parented, our experiences and the belief and values formed the approach we use when parenting.

Spouses come into parenting with different experiences, and this is often when conflict emerges where belief, values, and experiences differ. These differences not only strain their marriage, but it also confuses the children on the values and beliefs that they should hold.

Just like how children don't like being attacked, parents feel that their spouses attack their parenting style and make them feel like bad parents. While whether to take away too much screen time may not cause much harm, constant squabbles on how children should be disciplined can lead to behavioral issues in children.

Kids have to go through the different parenting styles and find a balance to avoid upsetting mom as they try to please dad. Either way, children feel the inconsistency is too much work, does not offer clear direction and confuses them which makes them unhappy. Some children who show aggression do so because of the weak link created by parenting styles. One parent may rule with a rod of iron while the other is permissive, or worse, parents may undermine each other's style in front of the kids.

The kids find the gap and exploit it to their advantage. While kids feel that it is working to their advantage, disharmony ends up being a disadvantage because boundaries and consistency make kids settle, behave better and are generally happier.

To create an atmosphere where kids thrive and grow, parents need to agree on the parenting style to use. If one parent is at home and the other at work, the parent at home makes the rules, and the other has to support and follow through. It would undermine a mom's authority when she announces bedtime and dad starts playing with the kids. This creates inconsistency for the kids and makes mom resentful.

How to harmonize parenting styles and discipline as a team

- Understand your parenting style

From the four parenting styles discussed earlier, understand if you are a permissive, authoritative, authoritarian or neglectful parent and see where your spouse fits. If you can, do this exercise together and help each other see where they fall.

Share your parenting philosophies and belief so that you understand where your spouse comes from. When you understand each other, you are likely to be more flexible and to make compromises for the good of your family and kids.

- Agree to disagree

Creating rules will mean that there will be agreements and disagreements and compromises to make. Agree on the most fundamental rules and handle the ones you disagree on one at a time. Rules such as bedtime, homework and playdate permission can create a balance before you agree on whether children should be given allowances and how much they should get.

Once the fundamentals are out of the way, a framework is created that makes it easy for kids to have balance and be happier. It also minimizes the chances of kids taking advantage and misbehaving. Once the rules have been set, ask for your child's opinion and allow them to contribute. Be democratic.

- Be a team

"Dad, please don't say, can I have another bowl of ice cream?" can lead to the answer "Let's see what mom thinks about it."

When kids are used to discord, they quickly learn which parent is likely to cave in certain situations. By noticing these triggers, involve your partner in the decision and then present it to your child as a united front. If your partner has already made a decision, back them up even when you do not agree with the decision.

Disagreeing with them in front of your child only creates more confusion for your child and causes resentment in the 'losing' parent. You can always ask your spouse about the decision later and discuss how such an issue is to be handled in the future.

- Be flexible

Parents are not perfect, and mistakes are bound to happen every once in a while. Blaming each other or fighting about it will only escalate issues without solving any problem. Find common ground when your parenting styles clash. Use creativity just as you would when your child misbehaves.

The bottom lines
When pregnant and a mom to be is asked whether they want a boy or a girl, the mom often answers with 'I don't care. I want a healthy baby'. While she may be hoping for a boy or a girl in the inside, parents first concern for their kids is their health. The moment you hold your baby in your arms for the first time, you have all these dreams for them, perfect score at school, the perfect mate, great career, and dream lifestyle, but amidst all these dreams, the one thing that parents want is happiness for their kids.

Employing the principals taught in this book; we take a step closer to helping our children achieve this happiness for themselves, and impart it on others. Deep down, people are communal, and we want to live in an environment where we are loved and accepted. We set them on a foundation to understand themselves, others and to be understood and accepted. A child raised in a positive parenting environment is likely to be happier, independent, creative, and confident when they are adults.

To truly have happy children, we must BE happy, allow our kids to be unhappy, give our kids more time than stuff, accept them for who they are, set limits, teach them to build relationships, and most importantly, expect effort, not perfection. It is unfair to put so much pressure on a growing child to be perfect. As long as they are making steps towards becoming centered, we are doing a good job.

Positive parenting is a journey. While it is best if you start when your child is born, it is not too late if you missed that bus. The idea is to catch up, be ready to do the work and follow through. When kids grow up, they won't remember what we said to them. They will remember how we made them feel, and when they remember what we said, it is because of how it made them feel.

Download the Audio Book Version of This Book for FREE

If you love listening to audio books on-the-go, I have great news for you. You can download the audio book version of this book for FREE just by signing up for a FREE 30-day audible trial! See below for more details!

Audible Trial Benefits

As an audible customer, you will receive the below benefits with your 30-day free trial:

- FREE audible book copy of this book
- After the trial, you will get 1 credit each month to use on any audiobook
- Your credits automatically roll over to the next month if you don't use them
- Choose from Audible's 200,000 + titles
- Listen anywhere with the Audible app across multiple devices
- Make easy, no-hassle exchanges of any audiobook you don't love
- Keep your audiobooks forever, even if you cancel your membership
- And much more

Scan the code below to get started!

BONUS

Thank you for purchasing my book. I have a gift for you. A collection of printable worksheets for your little children for FREE.

Click the link below

Reading list

Faber, Adele, and Elaine Mazlish. *How to Talk So Kids Will Listen & Listen So Kids Will Talk*, CPI Group (UK) Ltd, 2012.

Ginott, Haim. *Between Parent and Child*. New York: Three Rivers Press, 2003.

Kurcinka, Mary Sheedy. *Raising Your Spirited Child*. New York: Harper Perennial, 1992.

Siegel, Bryson Payne. *No-Drama Discipline*. New York, 2014.

Markham Laura. *Peaceful Parent, Happy Kids*. New York: Penguin Group, 2012.

Duhigg Charles. *The Power of Habit*. New York: Random House, 2012.

Conley Dalton. *Parentology*. New York, 2014.

Siegel, Hartzell Mary. *Parenting from the Inside Out*. New York: Penguin Group, 2004.

Chapman, Cambell Ross. *The 5 Love Languages of Children*. Chicago: Northfield Publishing, 2012.

PART 2

Positive Discipline for Teenager

Introduction

Adolescence is the moment when you realize that your little girl is no longer so little. These days, she prefers to dress like a rock star, wear tons of gothic make-up and loads of chains and bangles like rock stars do. She has even picked up playing the guitar, and the volume from her bedroom is unbearable. Your little girl rolls her eyes when you ask her to do something, never cleans her room (unless a friend is coming over) and spends half the day in her room with a 'do not disturb' sign on the door.

"Who is this person?" you wonder.

When she was born, your daughter, let's call her Jane, was delicate, adorable and the sweetest thing you have ever met. You did everything for her from bathing her, feeding her and clothing her. As she learned how to walk, you took her little hands in yours and helped her to gain balance just before you learned to let her go and walk by herself.

You created a safe environment for her to grow, move about, experiment, and learn. As she grew, you learned to move aside and give her room to move about freely while continuing to be safe.

However, now, you have a teen who is learning to be an adult, and it is quite understandable why things seem a little confusing. Your little girl has moved from being cute and cuddly to a gothic rock star fan. Why wouldn't you be worried?

What should you do now? How should you handle her development? Should you act out of fear and continue to protect and hover over your child? How soon should you let go and allow your child to master adulthood? How often should you offer advice (unsolicited or otherwise)? Should you report something to school when she shares it with you?

It is not surprising that, as a parent, you feel at a loss when you try to balance all these things. You know what your teen ought to do, but she doesn't do it. Moreover, to make matters worse, she does not seem to listen to your constant reminders and yelling, and any attempt to ground her is met with hostility, arguments, and bargains.

It's exhausting.

Something many parents do not understand is that positive parenting and understanding your teen's development could change this terrible, nerve-wracking years into a less stressful, more manageable period. Adolescence is a period where teens are learning to be adults. They are bound to fall and make mistakes, like we all do, and learn how to get up, dust themselves off and keep moving.

Your teen is likely to take on a new personality, sometimes every few weeks, as they try to identify who they are and get comfortable in their skin. It is a time of testing their limits, understanding themselves, and learning to love themselves. Believe it or not, your teen is just as confused as you are. Their bodies and their hormones are changing as well as their brains.

According to research, the teens' brain doesn't grow much during this time. It is already at 90% growth by the time a person is six years old. A thickening skull accounts for most head growth after this, but through adolescence, the brain of a teen undergoes remodeling similar to a network or wiring upgrade.

The principles of positive parenting offer a way out of this confusion for both parent and teen. Using the principles you will learn in this book, you will not only understand your not-so-little child more, but you will also be equipped with the skills you need to set limits, discipline and help your child become a responsible adult. This book will educate you and challenge you to support your teen in an atmosphere of mutual respect that affirms your teen's self-worth and as well as your self-worth as a parent.

Whether you have parented your teens with an iron fist or not, teens will love you for giving them more room to grow and make their own choices. They may misunderstand what this truly means, so it's up to you to help them understand the responsibility that comes with choices. Preparing your teen for life is your primary job as a parent, and this book will help you make the ride a little more enjoyable and stable.

Chapter one

What is Positive Parenting?

Liam has never been what you would consider being a 'bad child'. He was a normal child, but as he grew into his teens, he was not what you would call 'good' either. Instead, he was somewhere in between good, naughty, and bad. By the time he was 16, he was moody and detached completely from his parents.

He was not rebellious to your face, but he responded to his folks as he would any other teen. In simpler terms, he never spoke to his parents unless he needed something from them. As a parent, sometimes being ignored is worse than when teens are rude and unruly.

For years, Liam's parents had come to rescue him whenever he needed them to. As a little boy, they would rush to hold him when he lost a little balance and never gave him the chance to discover if he could regain it by himself. They had taken numerous trips to his school to 'iron out' issues when Liam was caught in the wrong, thus letting him get away with it. When they grounded him, he would retreat to his room and chat with his friends on his phone or play video games.

Liam got everything he wanted. His parents were eating out of his hands, and he knew it. For years, they had done everything they could to please him, and now, he did not respect them. Then the worst happened. Liam's mom arrived home from work and received a call from the police station. She was informed that some kids had been caught shoplifting, but one of them, her son Liam, had managed to get away. The sergeant was on his way to get him.

Liam's mother had two options. She was either going to let Liam take responsibility for his actions or speak with the sergeant to let it go, promising to take care of this on her own. She was at a loss. So, she called Liam's dad. After a lengthy discussion, the two had a plan on how they would handle things from now on.

Before we get to the solution, Liam's parent settled on, let us first consider the tell-tale signs that your child is now a teen. Besides the physical changes, are there any other signs you can look out for?

Some time back, a dad was horrified to discover over 150 messages his son had exchanged with a girl in his class. His son was 11 years old, and the conversation in the text was mostly about how much his son and this girl liked each other and their plans to kiss. He was perplexed. His older son, who was 16, did not seem to have that much interest in girls or texting, so it took him by surprise that his 11-year-old had become a teen.

Another parent was surprised when her 13-year-old daughter came down from her room with a face full of makeup. Her daughter had attempted to draw on her brows, put lipstick on, and had hurriedly applied blush. She did not know if she should take her with the makeup on or ask her to take it off right away and concentrate on her school work instead.

One mom's nephew never seemed to notice if his hair was combed or not. One day, he walked into the kitchen in sagging pants and shoes with shoelaces. According to him, he had mastered the art of teen look and would impress his friends if his aunty allowed him to maintain his unique look and style.

All of these are signs that your child is now a teen. Some changes can be described as more dramatic than others, but every change is met with an emotional response from you. The changes cause stress and anxiety, and as parents, we want to do everything in our power to protect our kids. However, before we can protect them, set guidelines, and give advice, we must first understand how teens are changing.

A Teen's Brain and how it Changes

The adolescent brain changes during their teen years more than any other time during growth. Research from the National Institute of Health has revealed that the brain undergoes a massive reorganization between the years of twelve and twenty-five. This conclusion was drawn after a hundred young people were studied as they grew during the 1990s.

Neurons use long fibers to send messages to other neurons through brain axons or long nerve fibers. The brain axons become insulated with a fatty substance called myelin. Myelin is the brain's white matter. It boosts the axons transmission speed up to 100 times faster.

Dendrites are branch-like extensions used by neurons to receive signals from axons. They grow twiggier and synapses grow richer and stronger. Synapses are little chemical junctions used by axions and dendrites to pass messages. Synapses that are not used a lot begin to weather, making the brains cortex thinner and more efficient. These changes make your teen's brain a faster and more sophisticated organ. This process of maturation was once thought to be finished by elementary school, but since proved wrong.

The slow physical changes move in a wave from the brain's rear to its front. This affects the brain's behavioral functions, such as vision and movement, to newer and more complicated thinking areas up front. The part that connects the brains left and right hemisphere, the corpus callosum, steadily thickens. Stronger links are also developed between the short memory directory (hippocampus) and the frontal areas where goals are set, and different agendas are weighed.

This results in teens being better at integrating memory and experience into decisions. The frontal areas also develop in speed and form richer connections, thus allowing teens to weigh far more variables and agendas than they did when younger.

If this development proceeds normally, teens get better at balancing their impulses, desires, self-interests, rules, altruisms, goals, and ethics. This, thus, generates behavior that is more complex and sometimes even more sensible. However, sometimes, if not all the time, the brain does this work clumsily and finds it hard to mesh all the cogs together.

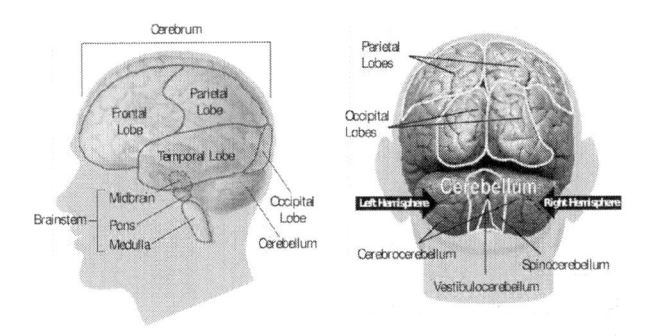

A while back, Becky, a mom to a teen, noticed her 14-year-old was not talking as much. It did not take her long to figure out that her daughter had gotten a tongue piercing. She did not like it, but every form of asking her daughter to get rid of it did not work. When asked, Lilly, her daughter, said that best friend had dragged her to get it.

"If you do it, I'll do it" was the dare that found Lilly in this situation, but her mother's nagging made her compelled to hold her ground. After a few weeks, when her mother had completely let the issue go, Lilly removed the piercing and the hole closed by itself. Her mother had attached the removal with an early Christmas treat, and Lily took the bait.

Beatriz Luna, University of Pittsburg professor, studied the teens' brains to illustrate this learning curve. Luna scanned the brains of twenty-year-olds, teens, and, children. She tasked this group with a sort of eye-only video game called an anti-saccade where they had to stop themselves from looking at a suddenly appearing light. The screen had a red crosshair at the center which disappeared as a light flicker appeared elsewhere on the screen.

The instructions were to look at the opposite direction instead of looking at the light with a sensor detecting their eye movement. It was not an easy task. Ten-year-olds failed 45% of the time. However, teens by the age of fifteen scored much better, almost as well as adults if they were motivated as they resisted 70 to 80 percent of the time.

The score was not the most interesting part of the experiment; instead, it was the brain scans that Luna took a keen interest in. Luna found that teens tend to make less use of the brain regions that monitor performance, plan, error, and focus, areas that adults engage automatically. This means that teens used fewer brain resources to resist the temptation to look at the light than adults who have all these other resources to use.

Teens used these areas less often and gave in to the impulse to look at the flickering light more readily, the same way they are more likely to look away from the road and read a text message while driving, even when they know they shouldn't. Once a reward was offered, however, teens pushed those executive regions to work harder, which thus improved the scores. By that age of twenty, their brains respond to tasks in the same way adults respond. Luna concluded that it could be a result of richer networks and faster connections thus making the executive region more effective, and this is exactly what Becky did to convince Lily to get rid of the tongue piercing.

This may explain why your teen behaves the way he or she does. They can be masterful on Monday, sleepwalk on Tuesday, disgusting at dinner on Wednesday and most cooperative before bedtime on Thursday. Along with the general lack of experience, your teen is also learning to use the new networks his/her brain is forming. Their brain isn't done developing, so expect them to do stupid things like tongue piercings, driving at 123 miles per hour and taking their eyes off the road for what they call a 'split second' to read a text message.

Now back to Liam.

By now, Liam knew that his mother was in the loop on what was happening. However, instead of the usual arguing, power struggles, and anger outbursts, she did something completely different.

"Wow! That was an interesting call. The cop will be here shortly. All the best Liam, I hope you have a plan on how you are going to handle this."

'Wait, what?' was the expression on Liam's face. His mother, on the other hand, was doing a jig. She had finally mustered up the courage to let her son take responsibility for his actions.

When the sergeant arrived, he had a long talk to Liam, and his mother pretended to feed the goldfish, who was more welcoming than Liam had been in a long time. The sergeant told her that he would need to take Liam downtown to which she replied with a mere, "That's ok. I understand."

Liam was baffled by now; he had no idea what was happening to his mother. She was calm and had no problem with him being taken to the station. Things must have been thick for him. She asked if she could talk to the sergeant alone and looped him in on what was happening. He agreed to help her out and was glad that she was not one of the parents who would follow him to the station and bail out their child as soon as they arrived.

Thirty minutes after they got downtown, and in Liam's presence, the sergeant called his mother to tell her she can come downtown and pick up Liam in an hour.

"I am a sorry officer, but I have other things I need to finish up." She told him.

"So, can you pick him up?"

"Not today, that's for sure. Maybe tomorrow after work or the day after. I have to check."

"We don't have any room in Juvie, so your son will have to be in an adult cell. We don't intend to scare you or anything, but we have picked up a few pedophiles and sex abusers, so they will be in lock-up with him."

"You do what you have to do an officer. I really can't make it today."

"Lady, do you know what could happen?"

"Officer, I am not the one who tried to swindle the mall. Liam made a couple of poor choices, but he is a good kid, and he sure is a tough one. I am sure he can handle it just fine."

At this point, Liam started wailing in the background. How could his mother not come and get him? Why was she neglecting her parental role?

"Mom, pick me up"

"Ok, but don't say I didn't warn you." the sergeant said as he disconnected the call.

Legally, Liam could only be held for three hours, so that's when his mother went to get him. He was pulled from a wooden bench where he had been sitting for three hours, and he ran to his mother and hugged her, thanking her for coming down to get him. Then he started to cry.

While a teen's brain changes in different ways and they not wired to use all parts of their thinking faculty yet, teens do hold the capability to push their brains by using the frontal cortex and making wise decisions. This is exactly what Liam's mother did. By pushing Liam to use his frontal cortex, Liam made the connections between his actions and the consequences he was going to face if he continued to make poor choices.

He also made the realization that his mother was not going to carry his responsibility for him or bail him out of trouble just because he was her son: his actions, his responsibility, his consequences.

Let us dive in a little deeper into how teen years change your child in terms of emotions and thinking.

Hormonal Changes in Teens and how They Affect Them

Teens are facing the emotional challenges of adulthood for the first time. How they process these emotions depends on how mature their brains are. As they grow up, hormonal levels begin to increase in areas of their brains that manage their emotions. The increase starts deep within their brains and slowly proceeds to the forehead where keys to decision-making are stored. This happens with time and maturity.

According to research, adults process emotions pretty differently from teens. For instance, when they see an angry face, multiple places in the brain turn on. One of the most significant areas is the limbic system, which is a small brain area where emotional processing starts. The prefrontal cortex, an area behind the forehead that plays a crucial role in making decisions, also comes online. The prefrontal cortex keeps unwise surges in check.

In teens, the limbic system develops quickly, but the prefrontal cortex does not. This leaves the emotion-processing centers hanging by themselves for a while. Teens engage the amygdala, an area within the limbic system, more when dealing with emotions such as fear.

To illustrate this, Tyborowska, a neuroscientist at Redboud University, recruited 14 year-olds for an experiment. During the test, each of the forty-nine boys and girls lay very still inside an fMRI scanner. These machines use powerful magnets to measure blood flow in the brain. Blood flow increases and decreases in different areas as the brain takes on tasks such as reading or managing emotions.

While in the scanner, each teen used a joystick to perform a series of tasks. While viewing a smiling face, the teen was initially supposed to push the joystick inward and push it away when they saw an angry face. After all, people are attracted to happy faces and will do anything to stay away from angry faces.

The next task was a little different. The teens were to push the joystick inward when they saw an angry face and push it away when they saw a smiling face. It is unnatural for people to approach something threatening, and it requires self-control. Teens needed to exercise emotional control to perform the task.

Tyborowska measured which parts of the brain were active during each task and the level of testosterone in each teen. This hormone rises significantly during puberty and is associated with muscles and size in make, but that's not the only area if affects. The hormone is present in both male and female and has an important role in reorganizing the brain during adolescence, controlling how the brain structure develops during this time.

The increase in testosterone is linked with how teens behave during adolescence. When they are forced to control their emotions, teens with less testosterone rely on their limbic system. This makes their brain activity a lot like that of a younger child. Teens with a lot more testosterone, on the other hand, tend to engage their prefrontal cortex to control their emotions and form a pattern that looks more like an adult using their brain.

Teens' brains mature differently, which is why it was important that Tyborowska had teens of the same age in his test. At 14 years old, some teens are relatively far in puberty, while others are not. Since the task was relatively simple, the teens performed both tasks equally well. More complex situations would be harder for a teen whose brain is still maturing.

That is why your teens will behave differently. One may be more rational while the other is impulsive. One may deal with bullying or a divorce better while another may sink into depression, finding it hard to handle tough situations. One may find it easy to fend off peer pressure while another will get a tongue piercing after a dare just because.

So, teens are not stupid, though they tend to do stupid things. If pushed a little to use their frontal cortex, a teen can be more responsible with their actions. It may not always happen, and they are bound to do stupid stuff now and then. However, when this happens, it is up to you as a parent to let them face the music. This wires off their neurons and creates the understanding that their actions are their responsibility.

They get to understand that you will be there for them, but you won't carry their cross for them. You may share advice and give suggestions on what they can do to make things work out, but you won't do it for them either. This communicates that you trust them to make sound decisions and, when they fail, you trust them to face the consequences and make things right.

Physical Changes and What They Mean to your Teen

A while back, you took a little boy or girl home, excited and happy they had finally joined the family. They cried when they needed your attention, and you attended to them with love and care. A few years down the line and they threw their first tantrum. It was as hilarious as it was annoying. You braved the years and set some ground rules, carefully allowing them to make some choices for themselves as long as they stayed within the rules.

During elementary school, you were friends. Your child would share their day's happenings with you, seek your advice, and hug you whenever they need comfort or just because they thought you were awesome. It was nothing but pure bliss.

But not anymore. Now they have mood swings, won't talk to you and would rather hang out with their friends than take that walk with you. You are just finding out that parenting a teen quite different from the experience you have had with them as a child.

Mary, the mother of a 14-year-old, was excited to go out after a long time. After she was ready to go, she went to the closet to grab her new $400 leather coat she had just bought. She could not wait to wear it for the first time. However, there was a problem; the coat was missing.

Mary knew where it was. It must be her daughter Kim who took it. They were about the same size, and Kim had formed a habit of borrowing her clothes without asking.

When Kim finally came home, Mary was stewing with anger. Just as she had thought, Kim had the coat, and it had a paint stain on the hand.

"Kim," she began, "why did you do such a thing! You knew that coat is new."

"It's not a big deal, mom." Kim retorted.

"Not a big deal! I just bought that coat, and now it has paint on it. How is that not a big deal?"

"It wasn't my fault. It was an accident. But if you weren't so stingy and bought me stuff, I would look good in I wouldn't have to wear your clothes!"

That was it. Mary was about to lose it, but she knew better. She knew she was too emotional to handle the situation, so she did something different.

"I am really angry right now, and I am in no state to solve this. I love you very much, and I choose not to argue with you over this. You wore the jacket without permission, and you have to find a solution for this on your own. Let's go to bed; we will discuss this tomorrow."

And with that, Mary heads to bed. She did not ask Kim about the jacket in the morning but waited for a talk about later in the day when she was sure that her daughter had done some thinking about the situation.

"Have you figured out a solution?" she asked her over dessert.

Kim sighed. She was used to her mother dishing out the punishment and taking whatever consequence her mother threw her way. Now she was put to task. She needed to solve this by herself.

"I don't know. Maybe you can ground me."

"That would not solve the problem, would it?"

"No, I guess it wouldn't."

Kim was silent for a while. She seemed to be thinking of a solution but coming out short.

"Would you like me to give you some options?"

"Yeah, I guess."

"You could buy a new coat."

"How much did it cost?"

"Four hundred dollars."

"Four hundred! I have no way of getting that kind of money? I don't have that kind of money."

"You could just forget about it then."

"And you'd never let me forget it. No way."

"That's true; I wouldn't. How about taking it to a leather expert and see what they can do?"

Kim thought for a while and decided that it was the best option available. The leather expert charged her fifty dollars, which she had to work for and earn in a week.

There are tons of reasons why Kim would have taken her mother's leather jacket without permission, but one thing is for sure, children change. All of a sudden, your kid does not look the same anymore. Kim used to be happy wearing a t-shirt and shorts, but now she wants to wear her mother's clothes all the time. She has even developed a personal relationship with every clerk at the mall, which often gets her bargains on the new arrivals so she can keep up with the trends.

Bodily transformation is so drastic in these five years. You son is towering over you and can easily lift you with one hand. Your daughter, on the other hand, looks good, really good, and with her sense of fashion, you are surprised your seed could look like that. It's as scary as it is exciting.

Like brain development, kids go through a more physical change in these five years than in any other time of their lives. They can think abstractly, but their hormones are causing changes unimaginable. They can grow a few inches a month, stagnate, then shoot up again without warning. Their bodies also produce more oil, which makes their face break out. The horror of dealing with a zit causes them sleepless nights.

Kids do not understand these changes (sometimes they don't even like the change) and mostly neither do parents. While the kids are changing, the parenting style you use needs to change accordingly if there is to be harmony at home. Parents face several challenges. Children in today's world are maturing at a younger age, and while the traditional family involved a working father and a homemaker mother to cater for the children's emotional needs, this model tends to be long forgotten and is only found in one out of four households today.

However, the extent to which teens have evolved is what parents have trouble comprehending. The homicide rate among teens, for example, is at an all-time high. Drug and substance abuse is another red flag. According to statistics, accidents that involved 15-20 year-olds reported that 29 percent of them were under the influence of alcohol.

An unacceptable number of teens drop out of high school, and an estimated 9.1 million STD cases are reported among teens. Teens say that their first sexual encounter was at the age of 17 or younger, and studies report that it is likely that teens will abuse alcohol or drugs before any sexual encounter.

No wonder parents are terrified. We can only remain hopeful that within the next few years, our teens will make good decisions in the real world. Speaking of the real world, the pressure and influence teens face now were unheard of in our times. Besides drugs, alcohol, and premarital sex, teens have to battle depression and suicide, which are battles that confront them every single day.

This pressure is overwhelming to parents as well, especially if we try to parent the same way our parents did a generation earlier. Parents no longer have that because-I-said-so control over their kids. Social, cultural, and technological revolutions have changed that. Children now feel that they deserve to be treated with respect and dignity and not be forced into autocratic control.

Besides all the changes that are happening, kids are struggling to find their place in the world. They are struggling to find out who they are and find their paths. Parents are stressed trying to work with their teens, and teens are stressed trying to figure out how to live with their parents.

Teens, Friends, and Parents

Noah was a good kid. He was settled, funny, and had what you would call a close-know friendship with a few friends. They had a lot in common and would spend most of the days together, playing, chatting, and helping each other with homework. As they grew older, Noah became more withdrawn, and he would hang out in his room by himself more than usual.

His appetite reduced, and he started losing weight. His parents were concerned about it and would ask him what was going on. He said he was fine and they stopped bothering him. Instead of nagging him, his parents decided to study his routine and see what had changed.

For starters, they noticed that his phone bill had gone down. Previously, Noah would text his friends so much and make such long calls that his parents would complain, but not anymore.

They also noticed that when he decided to talk, he did not mention his friends anymore. When they asked about it, he would seem to make up a story about it or shrug his shoulders before changing the topic or withdrawing again.

The problem was clear, Noah had fallen out with his friends, and somehow, he could not fix what had happened. What were they going to do to help him out? It was impossible to help him out without knowing what had happened, but if their son was to be happy again, a solution had to be found.

Teens are often warned of the impending danger of falling into peer pressure. However, research has proven that following the pack has some unexpected benefits for the teens as they grow into adulthood.

Three psychological scientists by the names of Joseph P. Allen, Bert N. Uchio and Christopher H. Hafen conducted a social experiment that proved that your physical health in adulthood could easily be predicted by the quality of close friendships in your adolescence. According to their results, remaining close to friends as opposed to separating oneself from their peers increases a person's physical health quality.

During adolescence, teens focus on forming and maintaining peer relationships, which may be an instinctive recognition that these relationships are vital for their well-being. Relationships they form provide some of the most emotionally intense experiences in their lives. It becomes easy for teens to conform to their peer norms even when it may be costly for them. The scientists suggest that social interactions may emphasize placing their peer's desires over their own but acting this way reduces life stress.

To test this hypothesis, Allen and his team recruited 171 seventh and eighth graders and studied them from age thirteen to twenty-seven. Each participant was asked to nominate their closest same-gender friend to be included in the study. Ranging from thirteen to seventeen years old, the participants best friends were required to answer questionnaires assessing the overall relationship quality. This included the degree of trust, communication, and alienation in the relationship. The friends were also to provide information about how much the participant forced themselves to fit in with their peers.

The participant's health was then assessed at age twenty-five, twenty-six, and twenty-seven with questions regarding their overall health, anxiety management, depression symptoms, and body mass index. Participants were also required to report any medical diagnosis and hospitalization to help account for any possible health problems.

From the results, it was found that people who had high-quality close friendships and a drive to fit in with their peers in their teen years had better health at age twenty-seven. This was also after taking into accounts other potentially influential factors such as household income, drug use, and body mass index. Adolescence relationships may come to influence an adult's health by later decreasing anxiety and depression symptoms.

Allen and his colleagues, however, were not the only ones interested in the study of teen relationships and their effects on health. According to another study collected from data correlating to 169 representatives, good friends make us happier in general. This study measured depression symptoms in teens while also investigating whether teens who were integrated into friendships had better mental health.

The youths were derived from different races/ethnic groups and came from household incomes ranging from $40,000 to $59,999. The teens were assessed annually and were expected to answer questions regarding their closest friends and the quality of their friendship. They also participated in interviews and assessments that checked feelings associated with anxiety, depression, self-worth, and social acceptance. Their friends were also interviewed and assessed.

A high-quality friendship was defined as a close friendship with a certain degree of attachment and support and an allowance for intimate exchange. The quality of a friendship was determined from the friend's responses. Popularity, on the other hand, was defined as the number of peers in a friend's grade who regarded the teen as a person they would like to spend time with. It was measured using nominations from all the teens participating in the experiment.

The study found that teens who had meaningful relationships had lower levels of anxiety and depression and higher levels of self-worth and self-esteem by the time they were twenty-five years old. The primary result of this experiment showed that teens who had previously been popular as adolescents had higher levels of social anxiety as young adults.

The lower level of anxiety and depression associated with strong friendships during teenage years was attributed to the positive experiences that helped boost positive feelings about oneself at a stage where personal identity is being developed.

Forming strong friendships is one of the most critical pieces of a teenager's social experience. The research also noted that being liked by a large number of peers does not necessarily translate into forming strong supportive relationships. Overall, when they are genuine and supportive, strong friendships in teens can foster high-functioning immune systems, lower rates of anxiety and depression, provide a longer life expectancy and build stronger emotional regulation skills.

To add to this, strong peer friendships can help build better self-esteem, happier and a more positive outlook on life even in the face of challenges, improve cognitive function, foster empathetic feelings and help teens gain the ability to cope with stressful events in their lives.

This study shows that Liam's parents were right to be worried about him. If teen friendships are so important, every parent would want their child to form healthy, strong, supportive relationships with their peers.

One day during dinner, Liam's mother decided to bring up the topic, but instead of directly asking Liam about it, she posted a general question that everyone would contribute to.

"Do you guys remember my friend Jane at work?"

Liam and his father knew Jane. She was Liam's mother's best friend at work and had been invited to a couple of family dinners.

"Well, we are having a bit of a thing, and I thought that you guys could help me get a solution. I would hate to imagine losing her as a friend, but it seems to be heading that way."

"What happened?" Liam's father asks.

Liam's mom continued to explain the situation. She had been working on a high-pressure assignment with her friend, and things started to go south when their boss seemed to favor her ideas over Jane's. When the boss was not around, Jane would make it difficult to agree on major decisions that were needed to move the project. They were late on their deadlines, and that meant they would get in trouble if a solution was not found soon.

"So, I don't know what to do."

"Have you tried to talk to her about it?" Liam's father asked.

"I have, but a confrontation has made her defensive, which is not solving anything."

"How about telling your boss about it?" he continued.

"That would get her into trouble, and the laws at our workplace are very strict for such cases."

"That seems like a hard place to be at honey. What do you think she should do Liam?"

For the first time, Liam was drawn in the conversation. He had been silent listening to his parent's talk. His teen brain was probably making dozens of connections on his situation with his friends.

"I don't know. I guess I would look for a time when we are both having a good time and bring up the issue or something."

Lima's parents exchanged looks. Liam had taken the bait. He had opened up about his friendship problem and found a way around it without them intruding on his privacy.

"I guess I could that. I could invite her to something we both enjoy away from work maybe."

"Like a movie, or ice-cream?" Liam's dad suggested.

"Or shopping. You like shopping a lot." Liam teased her.

"Yes, I do." She laughed. "Thanks, guys."

Without pushing it further, they changed the topic. That night, Liam offered to help with the dishes, something he had not done in a while. A few days later, Liam was back to himself, he was off to texting and calling again, probably having found a solution to his friendship problem, but something else had also happened. Whenever he needed help with his friendships, he was no longer afraid to ask. That simple dinner created a channel for him to feel safe and not judged by his parents.

Chapter Two

How Parenting Styles Influence Your Teen

When our kids are young, we must watch over them and do everything for them. When your infant cries, you rush to him/her and use your parental instincts, and some guesswork, to find out why he/she could be calling for your attention. Could he/she be wet? Is he/she hungry? Maybe there was a loud noise or a bad dream?

You were excited to record your baby's first steps, but once they learned how to walk, they were off, running around the house, only stopping to take the next corner to another room. They would dash off when she saw you holding clothes for them to wear and laugh heartily when you finally caught up with his/her toddler speed. You were always in pursuit.

As a toddler, he/she could not take care of themselves. They might roll down the stairs and hurt themselves, or miss a step and tumble over. It would be horrifying if he/she runs into the street, and with their current height, he/she can comfortably open the door and gate. The backyard is not as safe either. Who knows what insects and pests may be hiding behind the bush! A bite from god knows what is unimaginable. So, you followed them outside to keep them safe. Your toddler appreciated your being there, sometimes, because they knew that they would be safe as long as you had his/her back, literally.

Now as a teenager, they are off running again, this time in the family car with the keys in her hands, and they don't appreciate you following them around anymore. He/she wants to drive her own life and make her own decisions. He/she has abandoned post and prefers to hand out with her friends.

As a parent, you have to make use of these short teen years to prepare her to leave home. To leave as an independent person who can fend for themselves, make sound decisions, live ethically, and be responsible for their decisions and lives. The parenting style you use will determine how successful you become and whether or not you are going to have a good ride doing it, or hate every single minute of it.

The Fight for Control: The Drill Sergeant

As a parent, you may find it is easy to believe that it is your responsibility or part of your job to control your teen. You have to make them into what they need to be for their good. If you don't, you are a permissive parent.

Most drill sergeants often use punishment and reward as part of their parenting. They ground their teens, withdraw privileges, reduce or take away allowances, call names, and withdraw their love and approval. Gaining control makes them feel that they have done their job, but most drill sergeants do not take note of the long-term effects of their parenting style.

The teens, on the other hand, are discovering their autonomy, more like two-year-olds, and exercising their desire to take hold of their lives and be their person. They often feel that they have to give up themselves to be loved by you. They cannot make their own decisions because you will not approve, and if you don't approve, you will withdraw your love. They don't want that, so they try to fight with themselves and fail terribly, which only gets them into trouble.

Sometimes, to make sure they are getting the best of both worlds, they hide their stuff, sneak out, keep their lives at school and wear a different personality when at home. They negotiate for a reward whenever you need them to do something. If there is no external reward, they won't help out. They even try to manipulate you for a bigger reward through rebelling or complying.

You know this is not the principle you want them to adopt for the long haul, and frankly, most controlling sergeants get exhausted with this parenting style. They often feel like they are policing their teens, waiting to catch them doing something bad and dish out punishment or the all-famous lectures (monologues). When they catch them being good, they hand out a reward.

The teens learn a different responsibility: don't get caught, and if you do, it should be doing something good so that you get a reward. If the reward no longer matters, rebel, and refuse to comply.

Taking away power from a teen will not help them to learn responsibility. They will never learn by making mistakes and learning how to set their limits.

Teens like hanging out with their friends and Jacky is no different. Her father has given her permission to hang out with her buddies over the weekends as long as she gets her homework done on time. However, they have one major problem; Jacky will never keep curfew. It started as a five-minute extension, then it moved to fifteen minutes and, before her dad knew it, she was coming home later and later every single time she went out with friends, sometimes even a few hours after curfew.

As her parent, the father felt it was his duty to address this behavior. Every time she came home late, he grounded her for a week, and from then, a cycle formed. She would get out of grounding, come home late and get grounded again after a series of lectures on why she should come home on time.

When asked about it, Jacky's dad admitted that this did not yield much. As a teen, he would do exactly what his daughter was doing, and with time, he grew resentful towards his father and wanted nothing to do with him to this day. That is not the kind of relationship he wants with his daughter, but as a parent, he feels it's his duty not to let her get away with this kind of behavior.

What parents don't realize is that teens find grounding and taking away privileges as disrespectful and unreasonable. They view themselves as adults and would want to be treated as such.

Another danger that comes with controlling teens is rearing approval junkies. These teens know that they will only get what they want if their parents approve of their behavior. They get addicted to the approval and will look for someone to continue the job of controlling them when they are older. At work, their boss will have to control them. In a relationship, the role will have to be filled by their partner. Friendships are no different, as their friends will have to make the major decisions and essentially control them.

Some may become late bloomers and eventually get therapy where they can find support and learn how to grow and become their person. This is the very support that their parents did not offer. They never learned the skills they need to make their own decisions and be their person. It takes some time to convince them that is it ok to be their person and make a decision by themselves.

Drill sergeants eventually discover something: the world does not operate on a punishment vs. reward model. It operates on a consequence, and by punishing their teens, they are withdrawing the natural consequence that the teen needs to face for their behavior. If you don't perform well at work, your boss does not take away your car or your lunch break. You get fired. By knowing this, we think for ourselves and find a solution, thus why it is so crucial to show this to our children.

The Rescue Parent: Helicopter and Permissive Parent

The drill sergeant is often likened to a brick wall: rigid, rough, and sometimes sharp on the edges, easily cutting others. A rescue parent, on the other hand, is like a rag. They let their teens walk all over them, hide issues under the rug, protect to no end, spoil to unimaginable measures, and rescue their teens.

This parent feels that they have done their job because they have rescued and protected their teen from pain and suffering that would have been a result of their actions, thus robbing teens of an opportunity to learn from their own mistakes and gain life skills such as resilience. Instead of learning that pain and suffering can be survived, they grow up expecting others to serve them and end up equating love with the care they receive from others. They learn that they are weak and can't handle being sad, upset, or disappointed, and someone should always come and rescue them from the pain or they won't survive. They are incapable of doing simple, everyday things by themselves.

They become self-centered and believe that the world, and their parents, owe them something. They feel entitled to whatever they want and believe they should get it without earning it. This is inevitably transferred into the workplace, intimate relationship, and friendships. Their partner does all the emotional work as do their friends.

The rescue parent can also be likened to a helicopter. When there is an emergency, a helicopter hovers, vibrates and moves to the rescue. Emergency teams would not be operational without them. However, there is one problem: this being moving in to rescue when there is no real emergency. These are the parents who will drop everything to rush to the store or library to help their kid with homework because they did not have enough time to do it themselves.

They are the parents you see rushing in and out of middle school with science projects, trip slips and coats that their kids supposedly forgot about. They are waiting and watching for their beloved teen to send up a smoke fire so they can run to the rescue. They worry about their children's consequences when it should be the child shuddering over their actions.

They believe that they are involved in their kid's lives, and other parents may even admire them for it. Both the helicopter and permissive parent have one thing in common: they move to the rescue because they feel that their actions are out of love. They also tend to feel guilty for imposing consequences or allowing their kids to face the natural consequences resulting from their actions. So, when their kids get hurt, they bail them out. They steal their kid's opportunity to learn in the name of love.

There is another breed of helicopter parents who rush in with guns blazing ready to take down anyone who has inconvenienced their child. These parents will do whatever it takes to give their child the perfect life. These are rescue parents who rush in to help with the school project because it has to be perfect, but instead of helping, they end up doing the school project themselves.

Their kids' school transcripts have perfect grades, extracurricular activities, and awards that their kids did very little in earning. These parents often say that the world is competitive and would do anything to give their kids an upper hand, including bending the rules in the right way, but they forget that this is not how the real world works.

The drill sergeant and the rescuing parent are usually a cover for the emotional distance between parents and teens. The family may live in the same house, eat at the same table, drive in the same car, and be together on vacation, but they feel like a world apart. They may have a sense of something being amiss, but they can't place a finger on it or know how to articulate it. When the family interacts on rare occasions, it is either to rescue the child or to force the child into compliance.

The Consultant Parents: Positive Parenting

The drill sergeant grows tired eventually, and we all know a rescue mission cannot happen all the time. Even helicopters don't hover forever. The essence of this book is to look at a parenting style that works most of the time, that being the positive parenting style.

Your teen is growing, and as we have already explained, their cognitive development has changed to more abstract thinking. When kids are younger, they think concretely, which makes thoughtful guidance and sometimes firm limits necessary. However, a teen's thought pattern changes all of this. Their brains become drawn to pure emotion and thrill, but they also develop abstract thinking, which helps them escape the animal-like emotional reaction. They work more in developing their reasoning skills and the more advanced parts of their brain.

When they listen to the drill sergeant, all they hear is "You can't think for yourself; I have to do it for you" while the rescuing parent communicates "You are fragile, how can you make it without me?" This makes setting limits an issue of commands rather than guidelines that makes teens feel safe. These limits are often backed up with more commands, and when everything seems to fail, includes sternness and anger followed by a dishing out of punishment.

A positive parent, on the other hand, asks questions, listens to their answer, and offers choices, more like a consultation. Instead of telling their teens what they should do, positive parents put this burden on their teens to help them establish opinions within a safe limit by giving acceptable choices.

This prepares their teens for the real world by using the family set up to reflect the reality kids will experience once they leave the nest. These parents invite children to learn that freedom comes with responsibility and that mutual respect starts at home before it is practiced elsewhere. Kids learn and understand that mistakes are perfect opportunities to learn and that they are capable of developing problem-solving skills.

Teens need to learn that family members have their own lives to live and that they are not the center of attention. Instead, they are part of the universe, not the central focus.

Let's think of a business. Businesses often fire consultants to give them an outside perspective of what they can do to improve their operations and gain profit margins. The consultant is hired purely because of their expertise; however, although they are experts, they are not hired to boss the company around and tell them how to do business. Management would grow hostile to such a consultant.

Instead of dictating, consultants advise. They use phrases such as "I was wondering if operations would be more effective for you if …" As you may well know, a consultant's responsibility is not to make a client take their advice. If the client does not like the advice, they can choose not to take it, and there is nothing the consultant will do about it.

Also, the consultant is not responsible for what happens if the client takes the advice or not. The client will bear the consequences by themselves. If the company makes a loss following the consultant's advice, the worst that can happen is that the consultant gets fired or loses referrals. The consultant, therefore, happily gives up authority and responsibility that accompanies it. That is a huge advantage on the consultant's part.

It is rare to hear an eight-year-old say, "I need a therapist," but a teen will often seek out guidance and counselor if they feel they could use some advice. Like a business consultant, a guidance counselor or therapist does not give orders. They don't ground anybody, run to the rescue or shout at their clients because they are mad. They instead offer empathy and understanding.

Just like a business client, the client of a therapist expects good ideas from their guidance and counseling. A therapist gives their views while exploring those of their client. Therapists feel that clients are the captain of their ship. They have made mistakes in their past, and they are likely to make even more mistakes in the future. It is the nature of life. What they help their clients to realize is that the mistakes are not a failure, but a learning curve. They hope that their client will listen to them, but they don't require it. They only rescue the client by breaking confidentiality if the client is physically endangering themselves or those around them.

This is the same with positive parenting. As kids develop into teens, parents need to make the shift from being a guide to being a consultant. It is not an easy shift, and most parents find it difficult to settle with the idea that the teens can think abstractly and only need them to consult on ideas. Parents need to shift communication gears from "You better get your homework done" to "I'm wondering if you won't get into trouble if you don't finish your homework."

Like a therapist, you need to learn to ask your teen questions that are going to help them develop their abstract thinking. For instance, your teen has been invited to a party and, if you know anything about teen parties, there will be booze. As a parent, you may feel that is it your duty to rescue and protect your child from this kind of company, but they have already chosen to go.

Making demands, giving ultimatums, and sharing concerns may not yield much, at least not in the long term, but asking questions will.

"How will you handle it if the cops arrive, Tom's parent is not home, and there have been underage drinking at the party?"

Such a question is likely to get your teen thinking. Suddenly, they have to come up with an answer. We have to warn you, though, asking your teens questions in bitterness and accusation will not be effective. They will feel like they are on a witness stand and go mute. But when you ask questions in curiosity and honest interest, your teen is likely to open up.

While asking questions is a good thing, there are a couple of questions we have to warn you against. When speaking to your teen, or thinking of ways to guide them, here are some questions you should rephrase in yourmind before you start the conversation.

Question: How do I make my teen mind me?

Alternative: How do I help my teen become capable?

Question: How do I make my teen understand that no means no?

Alternative: How do I support my teen's development process?

Question: How do I get my teen to listen?

Alternative: How do I help my teen feel significant and that they belong?

Question: How do I motivate my teen to do what I think is best?

Alternative: How do I begin to honor that my teen has different ideas and the captain of their ship?

Question: How can this problem go away?

Alternative: How can I help my teen understand that mistakes are not failures? How can I help my teen learn from their mistakes?

Question: What can I do so my teen can do exactly what I say?

Alternative: How do I help my teen social and life skills such develop problem-solving skills and identify and communicate feelings?

One of the major desires of any parent is to raise responsible children who are equipped with tools that will enable them to make wise choices in life. Positive parenting is based on this principle. By using this principle, your teens are more likely to find encouragement from you instead of resisting your control. Teens will listen when they felt listened to and understood.

When you start using some of these principles, you are likely to feel uncomfortable. That is quite normal. The more uncomfortable you feel, the more you know you are on the right path. Controlling, protecting, rescuing, and punishing feels comfortable because that is the model we were brought up with. We are doing our jobs when we lecture, become stern, and withdraw privileges. However, what your teen is learning from the experience is not what you would want them to take to adulthood with them.

Sure, they will comply in the short-run, but eventually, they will develop semi-skills or no skills at all to deal with real-life issues, which is the exact opposite of what we want to achieve. Sometimes, your desire to relieve your teen's pressure for the moment may get in the way, but don't despair. Positive parenting will eventually become second nature.

Do Children Raised by Consultant Parents Still Rebel?

Many parents get the misconception that just because they have adopted the positive parenting principles, their teens won't make mistakes. On the contrary, children raised in a positive parenting home are more likely to risk because they have confidence in themselves. They will risk, rebel, and learn from their mistakes.

You need to understand and accept that no technique can tame hormones or change brain development. Teens have to be teens, and when their hormones start ranging, their developmental tasks will begin but don't panic. While this is not an easy time for parents, it's not an easy time for teens either. They are confused, questing many things and discovering even more.

But we can promise you is that your teen will feel freer to rebel under your noses rather than going underground or abusing their freedom once they go to college.

When you decide to change your parenting style, give your teen a notice. You will be changing your role dramatically, so keep our teen on the loop, so they know what to expect. Giving up punishment and rescue missions is a major change. Your teen will often try to guilt you for not rescuing them, or try talking you into grounding them instead of letting them face natural consequences.

Your teen will also watch to see if you will follow through. You might have made many pronouncements in the past that you did not keep, so expect them to watch you like a hawk. They will be interested in knowing if you are serious or if this will be a way to guilt trip you and use it as leverage.

What you should remember:

1. You can help your teen become self-reliant, responsible, and capable by using long-term parenting techniques.

2. Responsible teens are more likely to feel good about themselves and the decisions they make.

3. Whenever you are tempted to control your teen ask yourself, "will this work in the long run?". If the answer is no, switch to using positive parenting techniques.

4. Responsibility is passed on through convert messages that allow your teen to build their character on their strength.

5. Micromanaging your child's life may be more comfortable, but it does not grow responsible adults.

6. Teens should be allowed to own their problems and their solutions.

7. Thoughtfully surrender control and allow your teen to make their own choices, mistakes, and to learn from them.

8. Use thinking words to offer choices instead of fighting words. State what you will offer and allow your teen to decide if they will go with the options instead of dictating the offer on them.

9. Instead of rescuing your teen when she falters, empathize with her, and allow the logic consequence of the mistake to sink in.

10. Consequences don't have to be immediate, so don't feel pressured to come up with a consequence (punishment) in the heat of the moment.

Chapter Three

How to Raise Responsible Teens

Mia was sitting at registrar's office trying to angrily convince him why she should register for a class whose registration was already closed. She was furious; she could not understand why the registrar could not make an exception this once. She was failing terribly at making her case, and she did the only thing she knew would help. She called her father.

He was a lawyer at a big firm, and he had done everything in his power to make sure his daughter got an admission to the university. He had attended the orientation on her behalf and made it a point to find out whom to see to make sure she got in. Everything was arranged from the word 'go'. His Mia had to be successful.

When he finally picked up, Mia did not wait to speak to him or say hello. Instead, she handed the phone to the registrar and demanded that he talks to her father. He was going to straighten things out for her like he always did.

This may sound bizarre to some, but it is not an unusual occurrence in campuses today. A lot of young adults away from home for the first time are incapable of making decisions and solving problems. But how do young adults find themselves with such limited skills? Let us try to explain.

When growing up, there are things your parents did that you did not like. Some things you hated, some things you condoned and some things you swore never to let them happen to your kids. However, that's not the problem, at least not exactly. In a bid to treat your children better than your parents treated you, you end up denying your kids the very skills you should be teaching them. You buy them to stuff your parents could not afford, don't allow them to struggle, get disappointed, frustrated and uncomfortable because you endured that every single day of your life, and now you are stuck, or about to be stuck, with a Mia of your own.

What will a young adult like Mia do next when she gets stuck? Will she continue to call her father to bail her out of the credit card debt? Or ask him to talk to her boss, so she does not get fired? It's impossible to rescue your child all the time, but positive parenting principles can be used to teach teens responsibility and how to handle their problems to become the kind of adult you would want as a friend by the time they are seventeen years.

A Teen's Self-Concept

Christine's best friend approached her during lunch and whispered cheekily, "Hey Chris, I've got some cigarettes with me. Wanna join me and try one?"

"Sure, why not."

The girls giggled as they walked towards the back of the school. But as they walked, Chris was filled with dozens of voices in her head. For starters, she knew her mother would kill her if she ever found out. She was sure she would be disappointed and ground her for the rest of her high school years. Chris was also not sure if the cigarettes were something she wanted to try, but what would her best friend think about her if she did not join her? She had already committed to try it with her.

By this time, Chris' best friend was lighting the cigarette. She took a puff, coughed a little and gave it to Chris.

"Oh, she'll never find out, but is this want I want to do?" Chris thought as she took a puff.

Teens struggle with many things in their lives, and they don't understand many of the things happening to them. They will go through some pretty shaky times during adolescence, but this passes eventually. What should be important is that they gain strong self-acceptance that will get them through tomorrow and give them stability for the future.

Chris does not have the stability that her parents have with their marriage, career, house, and cars. She does not know who she is yet, but she is working crazy hard to find herself. She spends much time with her best friend shopping for short clothes, crop tops, jewelry, and talking about boys. She is proving to herself that she is not an extension of her home. She listens to her best friend's advice as she tries to prove to her that she does not always listen to her folks.

What Chris does not realize is she is still listening to somebody outside of her head. Her best friend's voice has replaced her parent's voice. The voice in her head offers a way out, a way to form a belief and value that will shape the rest of her life. The adolescence crisis is trying to figure out how to make the right choices without doing it to please their parents or their friends but to do it because that is what they want.

Some of the most important changes in any teen's life are the development of self-concept and new attachments. Young children are mostly attached to their parents, but teen's attachment increasingly grows away from their parents towards peers. A parent's influence diminished at this stage.

According to Rik Erikson's book "Challenges of Development", teen's main social task is the search for identity which can be summarized in the ability to answer one question: "Who Am I?" In the search to answer this question, teens may 'wear' different roles and often experience role confusion when choosing and balancing the identities they are trying out. They can take on negative and undesirable identities, try out some positive identities and sometimes even giving up on looking for identity if nothing is forthcoming. From this, Erikson developed eight stages of psychology.

1. Trust vs. mistrust

Infants from birth to twelve months learn to trust adults. This happens when an adult meets a child's basic need for survival. Kids communicate this through crying, which makes it vital for caregivers to attend to children when they cry. When a child's need for survival are not met, a child develops anxiety, fear, and mistrust.

2. Autonomy vs. shame and doubt

Toddlers from one year to three years learn that they can control their environments through their actions and get results. They show clear preferences for toys, clothes, and food. If denied an opportunity to work their environment, even when the clothes don't match, they doubt themselves, which leads to low self-esteem and feelings of shame.

3. Initiative vs. Guilt

Preschoolers between age three and six are capable of initiating activities and asserting control over their world. They do this through social interactions and play. They resolve this conflict by learning to achieve goals as they interact with others. Those who are not successful or are stifled by hovering parents may develop feelings of guilt.

4. Industry vs. Inferiority

Elementary school children (ages six and twelve) begin to compare themselves with others to see how they measure up. They become proud of their school work, sports, social activities, and family life if they feel like they measure up. They can also develop an inferiority complex during adolescence if they don't learn how to get along with others or have negative experiences at home and with friends.

5. Identity vs. role confusion

This is the stage we are majorly interested in. Beginning the age of twelve through to eighteen years, teens face the task of identity vs. role confusion. Their main task becomes to develop a sense of self. As they struggle to answer the questions "Who am I?" and "What do I want to do with my life?" Teens try on different personalities to see which one fits. They set goals, explore ideas and roles, and attempt to discover their 'adult' self.

Teens who are successful at this stage develop a strong sense of identity that they do not question in the face of challenges and problems or because of other people's perspectives. On the other hand, apathetic teens, those who don't search for their identities, and those forced by their parents to conform to their parent's idea of an ideal future develop a weak sense of self and experience.

As parents, we must realize that it is our kid's duty to identify who they are. Our role is to help them by asking them appropriate questions, setting expectations, and being empathetic. Teens who experience role confusion struggle to find themselves as adults.

6. Intimacy vs. isolation

As teens enter adulthood, they become ready to share their lives with others if they developed a sense of self. Unsuccessful teens may have trouble developing and maintaining meaningful relationships with others as a strong sense of self is critical in developing relationships. These adults may experience loneliness and isolation.

Even without going further into the eight stages of psychology, you can already see why teenagerhood is such a critical time in a person's life, and why the drill sergeant and the rescuing parent are setting up their teens to fail.

James Marcis developed an approach that can help parents better understand how teens choose their identity. Mercia asked adolescents questions regarding their understanding and commitment towards issues related to politics, sexual behavior, religion, and occupation. The results helped the researchers develop "James Maria's Stages of Identity Development."

Marcia used Erikson's notion of an identity crisis. In his research, he noted that adolescence was neither a time of identity resolution nor a time of identity confusion but more of a time for identity exploration and commitment. This exploration helps the teen identify a variety of life domains, in particular, religion, vocational, relational choices, gender roles, and many more.

Marcia identified two distinct parts: crisis and commitment. The crisis is a time of reexamining old values and choices which leads to a commitment made to certain role or value. Marcia identified four psychological development stages.

1. Identity diffusion

This stage refers to teens who have neither identified nor committed to any particular identity. These teens have not made any significant considerations of their identity. They are passively floating through life and are highly reactive. They avoid discomfort and seek out pleasure.

Jimmy is stuck in the identity diffusion stage. He just graduated high school, where he stumbled through his classes without a plan or a vision of the future. He has not applied to any colleges or vocational school and does not seem to be interested in applying. He works part-time at a pizza shop where he earns a little cash, so he has something to live off of. He does not earn enough to rent an apartment, so he lives with his parents, but he does not pay them any rent or contribute to any grocery shopping. He has not made any attempt to apply for a full-time position and any attempt his parents make to ask him what his plans for the future is are met with a resounding "I dunno" and general disinterest. He has no goal or plan and is floating through life.

2. Foreclosure

These have a low degree of exploration and a high commitment level. These teens are not trying to identify what is important to them or questioning the values and believe they have been taught. They accept the beliefs of their family and commit to them. Put, they passively accept the identity their parents choose for them and commit to this identity. While their commitment is strong and firm, they do not question why they are taught these values and beliefs or seek out an alternative.

One of these teens is Jasmine. She has applied to the college her mother and grandmother went to and has 'decided' to study elementary education like her grandmother. She has not given a thought to college or considered any other college she might like to attend. She has not even considered any other career options. Like most women in her family, she plans to teach for a few years and then stay home with her kids. She has accepted that she will be like other women in her family and does not seem to bother considering other options that would be available to her. Her goal in life is to proceed according to the customary path that women in her family have followed.

3. Moratorium

These teens are the opposites of foreclosures. They have a high degree of exploration with a low degree of commitment. These teens are in the midst of an identity crisis. They freely experiment and explore different values, beliefs, and goals. Making a final decision on any of these, however, is the problem. They have no clear value, goal, or guideline that steers their life. They are keeping their options open.

This perfectly describes Emma. She argues with her parents about going for Sunday service at the Anglican Church though she has gone to every Sunday service with them since she was a kid. Instead, she spends her time reading about different religions and spiritual belief. She plans to visit every temple and synagogue around to see how their Sunday services are and their way of worship. Sometimes, she questions religion altogether and wonders if God exists. Emma is not certain what she believes, but she is searching and exploring actively on the values, belief, and principles she wants to live by.

4. Identity achievement

These teens have a high degree of exploration and a high degree of commitment. These teens achieve their identity through a high level of exploration and make a high commitment to the values, beliefs, and principles they settle on. At this stage, teens will have decided which values and goals are most important to them, and what mission will direct their lives. They easily prioritize what is important to them and means that they have sorted through the numerous possibilities of whom they want to be. To achieve this level, teens must feel confident and be positive about their decisions.

Now back to Chris and what this means about her situation. Chris is about to take a puff of the cigarette, but before she does, she considers all the health benefits smoking would bring to her. She is knowingly risking her life and inviting lifestyle diseases such as cancer. She thinks about her studies and what it would means if she was caught with such a serious case in her final year in high school. It would ruin her chances of going to the college she wants. After making all the possible considerations, she hands the cigarette back to her best friend.

"I don't think we should do it."

"You are such a sissy." Her best friend retorts as she takes another puff.

Studies have assessed how teens pass through Marcia's stages and concluded that although teens eventually find their way to develop stable identities, the path is not always easy and there are numerous routes they can use to get to stability. Some teens will adopt their parent's beliefs or the first role offered to them while others will search and explore for themselves to see if there are more promising possibilities. Others may spend years experimenting with different identities before they choose one.

Teens may even maintain one identity at home and a different one at school as well as a different one at their part-time job and a different one with their closest friends. The majority are eventually able to integrate all the identities into a single self-concept and a comfortable identity.

During this search, teens relied on their peers to help them identify who they are. Tom, for instance, is a bright kid. In 8th grade, he enjoyed hanging out with the nerds and did almost everything with them. During the middle of 9th grade; however, he started hanging out with the cool kids while maintaining his relationship with the nerds. For a while, he hung out with some stoners just to get variety and even pierced a few body parts. He did all this while keeping his grades up, and now Tom plans to do his sophomore year in Singapore to get a better view of what he wants.

Judging from the people he hangs out with, Tom is trying on different identities. The cliques he hangs out with have allowed him to try on different personalities while still feeling accepted and significant.

Where do you go from here?

As teens explore different self-concepts and try to figure out where they should settle, they will make a lot of mistakes, and it is up to you as their parent to help them through. But how exactly do you do that without imposing your personal beliefs and values on them, hovering over them like a helicopter or rescuing them whenever they come calling?

This book has been written for this very purpose. So far, we have understood how teens change as they develop their thinking, the crises they go through as they experiment with different personalities, how their peers play into this role and the parenting styles to avoid. We have also looked at positive parenting and defined what it is. In the following chapters, we are going to marry all these concepts together.

Building your Teen's Self-Concept

Help teens feel good about themselves

Parent all over the world wants their kids to develop high self-esteem and high self-image. What most parents don't realize is that self-image and self-esteem cannot be developed by concentrating on it. Instead, they are a result of the way the home operates. When you encourage your child through consequences to make good choices, they naturally develop high self-imagine and high self-esteem.

Positive parents don't concentrate on talking about the importance of high self-esteem. They focus on being straightforward, thoughtful, encouraging, and empathetic. Parents can't pass on responsibility to their teens through lectures, threats, punishment, and intimidation. Responsibility and its components such as self-concept are passed on through convert messages that are geared towards allowing teens to strengthen character.

However, this does not mean giving children freedom and allowing them to get away with bad behavior either. As a parent, you have the right to expect good behavior from your children. Both adults and teens grow by building on their strengths, but it does not always work out that way.

Ask a teen what they are good at, and the majority will answer that they don't know. Ask them what their weaknesses are, and you might have opened a can of worms altogether. Teens are used to hearing their weaknesses repeated all the time.

"Your speech is sloppy."

"You can't even comb your hair right."

"Hold your pen properly, or your handwriting will look like a duck's."

This is not very different from what we experienced when growing up. What we should do is help our teens discover their strengths so they can build from there. It does not mean that we turn a blind eye to their weaknesses, but we should also not hyper-focus on the weaknesses at the expense of their strengths. Teens should work on their weaknesses as they build on their strengths. Don't overwhelm them by pointing out all the weaknesses they need to work on. Instead, let them work on one weakness at a time.

How to use Convert Messages

Whenever you speak to someone, you pick up on what they are saying and what they are implying at the same time. You are likely to pick up on what they are implying more than what they are saying. The same goes for our teens.

When you imply to them that they can't handle a task, they don't. If you send them a message that they can, their self-concept and self-esteem improve. If they receive enough of these messages, they feel good about themselves.

Let's imagine you have a really good boss. They are impressed with the work you perform, and they like working on projects with you. Your boss constantly sends you encouraging messages and only points at a weakness every once in a while. How would you behave around them?

Like most people, you will go out of your way to outperform the expectations set for you. You will do everything you can to meet deadlines, perform research in an exemplary manner, and compile in-depth data to support your hypotheses. You would hate to disappoint your boss, and you would work extra hard to make sure the rest of the team works in harmony to get the job done and not pull you behind.

Now, remember being around someone who thought you were the scum of the earth. They approved of nothing you did and never gave compliments. How did that make you feel? Did you want to be around that person? What was your response?

Teen parenting works the same way. What we imply to our teens matters more than what we say. We must imply that we know they are going to handle whatever life hands them, then trust them to live up to that expectation.

When your teen wakes up in the morning, what message does he/she send herself? When he/she looks into the mirror, what do they see? A teen who looks at the mirror and sees a positive thing, someone others would like to be associated with is likely to better mannered than one who looks at the mirror and is disappointed at what they see. The messages you send your teen will either make them rebel or invite them to comply with you.

Responsibility and Self-Concept

Your eighteen-year-old just entered college, and he is excited to attend his first party. He calls you and lets you know he will be going to a party, and although you are miles away, you remind him of why that the university has a rule against sex in the dorm. You also tell him that he should be home by midnight, not a minute later.

At midnight, he has met this amazing girl who is on his arm, and beer is being passed around. Everyone around him, including the girls he just met, is encouraging him to continue drinking. In this instance, the rule that the college is against sex in the dorm does not make sense at all. As if that's not enough, he has never had the opportunity to listen to the voice in his head and make a decision by himself.

Meaningful and mature behavior stems from within. When teens learn to make decisions and live with the consequences, their character is formed. When they were younger, we could get away with making decisions for them, but as they grow older, making decisions for our teens hinders them from growth. We must learn to share control with our teens by helping them to think for themselves.

Later the following day, your son calls you with a problem. He has been arrested for being intoxicated in public. This happened when he was escorting the girl from his dorm. He can't even remember her name. At this point, you have a choice to make. One choice is you can tell him how mad you are that he disregarded your advice and now you have to spend fifty dollars for his court case and fine and still buy him the books he needed for school.

Alternatively, you can realize that your son is now on his own and he needs to be responsible for his decisions and face the consequences and respond with "I am really sorry about what happened. I am sure you really needed the money for your books instead of pay that fine, but I am sure you can find a part-time job to make it up."

Let Teens Own their Problems

Allowing teens to own their problems and solutions helps them build their self-concept. As parents, we help our teens make decisions and allow them to own the good and disappointing feelings that come from the choice. This communicates that the quality of their lives will depend on the choices they make. We must also make it clear who owns the responsibility for a particular problem. We should let them own the problem, their own feelings, and their disappointment and reward. We should not give the message that kids shouldn't do something because it will make us mad or sad.

This encourages them to shape their choices around the voices outside their heads or reinforce an immature rebellion to make us mad. In both cases, the teen does not own the responsibility for the problem. Let's say your son's friend plans to sneak out of school for the afternoon to hang out at the mall. Would it be better if he thinks "Boy will my dad be angry when he finds out" or "The teacher is introducing a new topic today, so I better stay behind so that I don't miss it." If he is a sensible young man on his way to healthy self-concept development, he will stay in class.

Instead of solving the problem for the teen, we should give back the responsibility for the problem with empathy. For instance, you can tell your son, "Oh bummer, that must feel lousy." He feels that you empathize with him and understand how he feels, but you have not solved his problem.

Telling teens that they are good will not build their self-concept. While positive reinforcement works with teens who feel that they are a 10, most teens feel that they are not even close to a 10. If a teen has a poor self-image, they will simply discount what you say and probably end up worse than they were initially. To help them build their self-concept, we must talk to them as we would adults by criticizing them as little as possible while still allowing them to think for themselves and make discoveries. This can be easily done by asking them questions instead of ordering them around.

When your teen says they will do something stupid, respond by telling her "Well that's an opinion. Have you thought of this, this and this? We will still love you regardless of what choice you go with."

Neutralize arguments by keeping the focus on your teen.

Any attempt to use positive parenting short-circuits the minute you enter into an argument with your teen. Arguing and entering into a reasoning contest with your teen is fighting a war you will never win. You will become exhausted and eventually give up. Your teen, on the other hand, will become emotional, likely angry, and stay that way until they have had time to cool off.

To neutralize an argument with positive parenting principles, you should use genuine empathy to soak up emotions. For instance, you can say, "I love you too much to argue about that. Let's have some time to calm down and talk about it later."

Empathy should come from the heart. You can use a statement that comes naturally to you. It can even be the same one every time, accompanied by the same facial expression and body language. This will give it a cumulative effect.

Chapter Four

How to Connect with your Teen

During the teen years, your children will not want to spend as much time with you as they learn how to form connections with people outside the family, but this makes it vital for you to connect with your child and spend time with them.

Connecting and spending time with them does not mean the usual time you see them in the evening or at any other time. It means scheduling-in special time with your teen like you would a business meeting. This time should be as sacred as a million-dollar meeting. Unfortunately, on their busy schedule, your teens need to spend more time with friends rather than the time spent lecturing, punishing and judging. However, even with the hustles and bustles of life, parents need to realize that sometimes, you get more results when you ignore the behavior and concentrate on building a strong relationship.

It is heartbreaking to learn that your teen is experimenting with drugs and alcohol, and Jenny was not happy when she learned that Sam had been caught smoking again at school. If she continued like this, she would not graduate high school. Sam was a good kid most of the time, but her experiments with drugs and alcohol and open defiance of her mother were getting out of hand.

Jenny did what she knew best: she grounded Sam and took away her car, phone, and desktop computer until she straightened things out, but that did not stop Sam. She continued with her wayward ways and started coming home late, sometimes smelling of booze. Jenny was devastated. Before heading over to Sam's school, she passed by her friends place to offload and try to figure out what could she could do. Maybe someone on the outside would give her a different perspective.

"How is your relationship with Sam?" her friend asked after Jenny explained the situation.

"Huh! Relationship! Do we have one?"

"Why don't you ignore her behavior and work on your relationship instead. Connect with her and get to know her?"

"How will that help the drug problem?"

"It probably won't help, but when you know her better, you will be in a better position to address the drug issue. What do you think?"

"I am not sure it will work, but I have tried everything so I might as well try that."

After a chat with her friend, Jenny went to Sam's school and talked with her teacher. They had a long talk as Jenny told the teacher her new plan and asked the school to give her a little time to work things out. Sam's teacher agreed on the condition that if Sam didn't straighten out her grades, she would be expelled.

Without another word to Sam, they went home. Sam was suspicious. She expected the ride home to include lectures that would be continued over dinner and come up over the next few days. She was not sure what her mother was thinking, so they kept quiet.

When they go home, Sam could not contain herself.

"I guess am grounded, huh?"

"No, not really."

"Mom, are you ok."

"Yes, I am. Look, Sam, you have made some poor choices lately, and it's a bummer, but you are the one who will have to live with the consequences of your choice."

The following day after school, Jenny pulled up at Sam's school just in time to catch her.

"Wanna grab some ice-cream?" she started.

"Ummm, ok," Sam answered, suspiciously.

Sam did not say anything the whole time. They had their ice-cream in silence and went home. Jenny told Sam it was nice spending time with her. Sam was still suspicious, but she went along with it and said it was fine before she retreated to her room.

Over the next few weeks, Jenny took Sam out for ice-cream every Tuesday after school. Sam started to open up after a while and began to share a little about her day. Within a few weeks, the pair enjoyed their Tuesday ice-cream treats, but one Tuesday afternoon, Jenny didn't show up. She got held up at work and could not make it.

"Mom, what happened today?"

"Sorry sweetie I didn't know you were expecting me. We never said this would be a regular thing, but I would like to make it regular if that's ok with you."

"Yes, I'd like that."

"I will leave a message if I get held up again."

A lot has changed since Jenny introduced this routine. Sam helps more at home, and her grades have taken a turn-around. She comes home early and even invites her friends over. For a few weeks now, Jenny has not smelt beer on Sam. By connecting with her and creating an atmosphere where Sam could think about how her behavior was affecting the rest of the family, Sam stepped up and took responsibility for her problems and consequences.

Here are some ideas on how to connect with your teen and spend time with them:

Teens and parents are different, so finding something that will work for both of you is vital. Your teen may not enjoy ice-cream but may have a ball bowling or ice-skating. Here are a few ideas to consider.

Listen, don't judge

Let them choose bonding activities

Invite them to see you at work

Join them for their favorite TV show

Take walks together

Include them in your discussions

Be available, set your work aside to spend time with them

Cook together

Ask for their opinion

Trust them

Support their interests

- Validate their feelings
- Stop nagging, punishing and controlling
- Enjoy their taste in music
- Take a trip together
- Share about yourself (when they are interested)
- Let their friends feel comfortable to come to your house
- Try a DIY project together
- Go to a concert together
- Ask for their help
- Laugh together

Spending time with your teen gives you an opening to understand things from their perspective, get a glimpse of their world, and bring back the joy of parenting. It takes real effort and a conscious decision to make it happen. No matter how busy you are, spare time for your teen and see how much your relationship grows, how strong their self-concept becomes, and what a great ride you both get.

How to Listen to Teens and Finally get them to Listen

Penny, 16 years old, had not cleaned or tidied her room in a few weeks. Every time her mother, Anna, went to put the laundry away, the previous day's dirty clothes met her on the floor. The situation had gotten so bad that Penny was not changing her underwear or taking a regular shower. Anna talked to her (lectured, nagged, reminded, threatened, coaxed), but nothing worked. Penny just wouldn't listen.

Like Anna, when most parents hear the word communication, what comes to their minds is talking, which we have already defined in 'parenting terms' as coaxing, nagging, threatening, and lecturing. However, have you ever looked at your teen when you are 'communicating'? Are they listening to you or rolling their eyes, texting a friend or glued to the TV? They might be singing their favorite song in their head to block out everything you are saying.

If you feel ignored when you talk to your teen, chances are you are being ignored. There is no question about it. If you ask a teen what you just said, they will incoherently mummer two or three things and tell you they heard you. Usually, it goes something like "Fine; I'll clean my room, empty the trash, and help out around the house."

Then the routine continues. This is exactly what was happening to Anna and Penny. Things had gotten so bad that whenever Anna brought up the topic, Penny would tell her it's her room. She shouldn't even enter it in the first place, and if it bothered her so much, she should just keep out. Anna was vexed, so she stopped doing laundry for Penny. If she was such a big girl, she should take care of laundry herself. Penny was not bothered. She just repeated what was not too dirty and cleaned a single top, dress, or trouser when she wanted to wear it the following day.

When parents complain that their teens don't listen, what they mean is that their teens are not obeying them. Amidst all the nagging and lecturing, parents fail to realize that the first ingredient of communicating with teens, and anybody else for that matter, is listening. Before you complain that your child is not listening, check whether you have modeled how to listen.

With so much information available on listening, you would think that many parents and people in general, would know how it's done, but that's not the case. Issues keep popping up, and since people take what they hear personally, they are usually at the battleground ready to defend their position. Parents tend to get ego involved with kids.

"I am the parent you should obey me."

"My house my rules."

"I am teaching you how to be a good citizen."

"It's my job as the parent to teach you how to act responsibly."

Even when talking does not work, parents still imagine that somehow it will get through their teen's thick skulls and they will fall in line. Without realizing it, parents block communication by not listening. Here is how they do it:

1.   Rescuing their teens so they can be good parents instead of letting their teens figure things out.

2.   Downplaying a teen's feelings and perceptions, so they have the right feelings and perception.

3.   Defend your explanation and point of view when your teen does not accept it as gospel truth.

4.   Interrupting their teens to teach a lesson on morality and values.

5.   Letting personal issues get in the way and interrupting their teens when they say personally.

6. Using your teen's words against them to criticize, lecture, and name-calling.

You can't talk and listen at the same time, and you can't be thinking about what to say next when listening to your teen. The same way teens watch TV or text a friend when you are talking, that is what you do when they talk, and you're thinking of what to say next. The best way for parents to learn how to listen is to get tips from their teens. Jane Nelsen and Lynn Lott, in their book "Positive Discipline for Teenagers," asked teens for some tips on how parents should listen. This is some of the tips they gave:

1. Stop lecturing.

2. Keep it short and sweet.

3. Listen to teens instead of talking over them.

4. Stop repeating yourself.

5. Don't overreact when they get the guts to tell you what they did wrong. Don't be mad either.

6. Stop making promises you can't keep.

7. Stop guilt tripping teens by saying things like "I did it because you did not have the time to do it."

8. Stop yelling from a different room and expect them to come running.

9. Don't talk to their friends about them.

10. Stop prying and giving teens a third degree.

Nelson and Lott gave four tips to help parents listen better.

1. The feeling behind what you do is more important than what you do. Reading the paper while you are listening or thinking of what to say won't cut it. Always have open body language and genuine interest in what your teen is saying.

2. There is more than one way of seeing things, and parents often block out every other way and hold on their perspective. From now on, have respect for open realities. Your teens love it when you have an interest in them.

3. Be empathetic and mean it. Saying "I can understand why you might feel that way" in a sarcastic way or part of defending your point of view is not showing genuine empathy. Say in a way that shows your teen that you truly understand how they could have come to that conclusion.

4. Be curious and ask questions that will invite your teen to give you more information. For example, how did that make you feel? What part of that was most important to you? Is there anything else?

Anna finally gave up. She stopped nagging, threatening, and lecturing. Instead, she started being interested in Penny's stories and programs and guided her without judgment on other areas. She completely stopped asking about her untidy room or dirty clothes. She found her interesting, and when Penny had a big test coming up, Anna would help her with the laundry, so she had more time to study. One day, as she was busy cleaning the house, she realized she had not seen Penny in a while. Teens will be teens, but she thought it might be a good idea to check on her.

When she got to her room, Penny was busy cleaning up. Her bed was made, fresh sheets and all, her books were arranged, and some of her things were in a big box written donation on it.

"What's going on?"

"Nothing, I'm just cleaning. Do you think red would be a good color for my room? I have been saving up for some paint in the last few weeks, and I am ready for a new look."

Help your Teen Communicate their Feelings

For the longest time, parents have been lecturing and using words that don't show their teens that they understand their point of views, but you can learn to communicate from your gut and heart by feelings words. Instead of hiding feelings, you should help your child understand and communicate their feelings. However, most parents don't name or express their feelings, which makes it even more difficult to deal with the burst of emotions teens have.

Even worse, most of us were brought up by drill sergeants who did not care about our feelings a lot of the time. We became out of touch with feelings and had no background on how to help our kids with their feelings since we were not helped with ours. But it's not too late for us, and it's certainly not an excuse for not helping our teens communicate their feelings.

To make it easier, let's divide feelings into two parts: feelings that come from the gut and feelings that come from the heart. Love, loneliness, compassion, and empathy are feelings from the heart while courage, fear, honest are feelings from the gut. In some cases, judgment from your head will serve communication better than any of these feelings. This is called listening to your head. The solution to most communication problems is to identify the barrier and find the appropriate balance.

A few weeks after Penny had started cleaning her room, she started messing around with boys. After she started taking care of herself, boys started noticing how pretty she was. The attention felt good, but she was not sure how to talk to her mom about it or if she should at all. As a young girl, having a few boys interested in you is great. She dressed better, took care of her hair, and even applied to makeup with care. Anna was tempted to go back to her default setting of arguing, controlling, and threatening.

Their relationship became superficial, and although they spent time together from time to time, it always felt like something was missing. One day as they drove home from a movie, Anna noticed that Penny was anxious. She on the fence with something, so Anna decided to go first.

"I feel really bad about the gap in our relationship. I love you, and I know you love me, but lately, our relationship is more superficial. I really wish there was something we could do to close the gap."

"I don't want to talk about it." Penny relied on.

"I think I am a better listener than I was a few months back, and I have learned a lot during that time. I used to think I know how to listen, but I was wrong. Please give me a chance."

Penny took a moment to think about it before she started talking. She was confused by all the attention she got, and she did not know what to do about it. She had no experience choosing a boyfriend or what you are supposed to do with one. Some of the girls were jealous, so the attention she got came with a few enemies. She did not ask for it, and frankly, she just wanted to be free to be herself and to interact with other girls without feeling the pressure that they might hate her because she is pretty. It was an exciting world as it was confusing for her.

"And now I feel under a lot of pressure to live up to everyone's expectations. I have to dress in a certain way, behave in a certain way or people will be disappointed. It's too much. I can't keep worrying about my grades, boys, and what everyone else thinks. Why can't they leave me alone!"

"I understand why that would be much pressure for you. It's a lot for one anyone to handle. What are your thoughts about it?" Anna asked.

"Well, there is this girl from last year who was more like me. Like a hidden flower that suddenly blooms. She had to drop out of school because she got pregnant and I don't want to make the same mistake. I never realized how serious life is until I cleaned my room. I never really took anything seriously before that because life seemed like a game. Ever since I cleaned my room, and I started getting all this attention, I realized things were not what I thought they were. Life is pretty serious, and I'm the one in control of mine. I have to make decisions about my studies, drugs, boys, and what I want to do for the rest of my life."

As Anna continued to ask curious questions, the barrier between them was broken, and their relationship was healed. Anna connected with Penny by listening to her, and their relationship was not only healed, but also made stronger.

The Fight for Control and How it can Foster Connection

Julia was furious with her mother. She said that her mother treated her like she was two years old most of the time, but also sometimes like the fourteen-year-old she was. When her clothes, friends, and homework were involved, she was a fourteen-year-old, but when boys are brought into the picture, she suddenly became a two-year-old. Her mom tried to control which boy she will talk to when she agrees at all, and whether she will go for a date or not.

Her mother, on the other hand, says she does this with good reason. The young men Julia is interested in have weird haircuts which her mother feels is bad company for her. This is just one area where parents and teen fights for control. As a parent, you may feel that one this is not too consequential while another is, which prompts you to tighten the belt and try to gain more control.

It is not surprising to find parents thinking, "I would be a better parent if I could control..."

However, that's not how human beings are wired. We have free will, which gives us the right to make decisions and live with the consequences. If we want to raise teens who are reasonable, responsible, and fun to be with, we must learn to share control with them by gradually loosening our grip on control. They will be out of the house in a few years so the more control we learn to give them now, the more they learn, become responsible, and surprisingly, the more connected our relationship with them becomes.

According to Sylvia B. Rimm, a psychologist, people compare the amount of control they have with the amount of control they used to have, not with the amount of control they feel they should have. The more control they gain, the more satisfied they are, and when it's cut back, they become angry.

When we first bring our kids home from the hospital, we have full control over what they do, but as they grow, we learn to let go and trust them to walk carefully, choose what to wear and other 'harmless' choices. Ideally, we should continue to loosen the grip as our kids grow into young adults, but most of us tighten the grip. No wonder the fight for control will never end. Teen's misbehavior does not help, forcing us to clamp down on them and keep fastening the belt.

For positive parenting, we advocate that you stop being greedy with control. Don't take more than you need, and frankly, as kids mature, the less it is. When you feel a battle looming, ask yourself these questions: "How much control is necessary to maintain in this situation? Will my teen learn a valuable lesson when we engage in a control battle or when I give them my opinion and allow them the space to choose?"

As a positive parent, you will learn that the more you loosen the grip and relax, the easier it is to deal with control. Instead of entering into a control battle, use positive parenting techniques to push your teen to think about their decision. Whenever you give a rule you can't enforce, you lose your teen's respect. For instance, you can tell your son not to hang out with a certain boy at school, but you can't be in school to enforce the rule. This is a battle you will inevitably lose.

Teens have a way to make you fight such a battle. As a rule of thumb, avoid control battles at all cost, especially if you know you are bound to lose. You will not avoid the battles all the time. There will always be those instances where you will find yourself in control battles. In these instances, win at all cost. As a parent, there are a few issues you must have control over at all times.

You must insist that your children respect you at all times. When a child disrespects you, it lowers their self-image. Insist that they respect you at all times. You must also have control over basic family conduct. For example, a teen should not be allowed to smoke in the house at the discomfort of other family members. As a parent, you must also have control over the home environment. Your teen should not be allowed to bring whomever they want and act as if they own the house. When they grow up and have their house, they will exert control over that environment.

To be an effective positive parent, you need to be thoughtful about control by offering your teen choices. The best time to give choices is when things are going well. When teens were toddlers, we would ask them if they wanted to have milk or juice. As teens, you can practice asking them if they want to be home by 10:00 or by 10:30 pm. You should be ok with the choices you give and be able to enforce them.

Brace yourself though. Most teens will come up with a third choice, and you are likely not to like it. Usually, the choice is the most common combination of "This is my home, too, I have rights, and I live here." When this happens, ask them, "What were the choices?" It does not matter what response they give after that. Simply continue asking, "What were the choices?" in a calm way. After four or five times offering the same response, you will have successfully driven your teen crazy, and they will behave after being obligated to make a choice.

Refrain from giving choices with the condition that teens must choose your way or suffer the consequences. For instance, you can either do your homework on time or lose your right to screen time." You must also offer reasonable choices. For instance, "Would rather clean your room now or in the afternoon?"

How to use Mistakes as Opportunities to Connect and Learn

Teens are bound to make mistakes. It's part of the learning process, but mistakes have such a bad reputation. For most people, mistakes mean that you are incapable, and that is what our teens grow up learning. This is mostly shaped by the negative messages parents give their kids. The numerous warnings and threats when kids are exercising their curiosity, and the many warnings of impending mistakes all communicate that mistakes make you incapable.

Parents have a crazy notion that for teens to do better, they must first feel bad, but people cannot feel bad and learn at the same time. Mistakes happen without warning, but teens can learn from them. It is hard to watch our kids make mistakes, so we must decide to be the positive parents who show them support when they mess up instead of making them feel guilty, shame, or punishing them.

One of the mistakes parents make is to talk, talk, talk, and tell their teens what happened. When a teen makes a mistake, you tell them what happened, why it happened and what the consequences are, and how they should be doing things to avoid the mistake. We might even add punishment to make sure the lesson sticks and our teens never repeat the mistake.

When your teen comes home with an outrageous announcement, take a deep breath before you rush into the usual "Oh no you won't need routine" And ask more curious questions like "Tell me more about that. Why do you think about smoking marijuana?"

Son: All the kids are doing it, and it seems like they are having a great time.

You: What do they say about you now that you don't smoke marijuana?

Son: (thinks for a while.) They tell me that they admire me and that they are proud of me.

You: Don't they try to pressure you to join them?

Son: No, not really. They usually ask me if I want to try it, but they don't pressure me to do it. I am just curious and want to try it.

You: What do you think your friends will say after you smoke some marijuana with them?

Son: (thinks about it for a while) They will probably feel disappointed.

You: How will you feel about it?

Son: (long pause as his thinking wheels turn.) I'll probably feel like a loser. Maybe I should not do it.

Not all cases will be this smooth. Some teens are actively searching for their identity and will end up smoking bang, even after asking curious questions and helping them determine that this is not a very good idea. Regardless, curiosity questions help kids think for themselves instead of hiding and rebelling.

Curiosity questions work best when you are actively listening because this is when you are genuinely curious about feelings, what they are thinking, and what they are learning. The more you learn about your teen, the more you can connect with them and strengthen your relationship.

Once a mistake has been made, help your teen model how to learn from the mistake instead of feeling that they are a failure. The best way to do this is to demonstrate how they can recognize the mistake, take responsibility for it, reconcile with themselves, and make a resolution.

Recognition means being aware that you made a mistake. Responsibility means that you have to be honest about the part you played in the mistake. Recognition means telling your teen how sorry you are for treating them disrespectfully or unfairly. Resolution means you are willing to work with your teen to find a solution that will be acceptable for both of you.

To effectively do this, don't focus on the mistake, help your teens evaluate their thoughts and feelings about the decision they made and what they will do differently next time to get a different result. Remember to treat your teen as you would like to be treated (with understanding, respect, and dignity), share what is important to you and why it is important and be flexible and make exceptions in some rules.

Let us recap what we said in this chapter.

1. Connect with your teen by spending time with them where your full attention on them. Make a special plan and treat this time like a million-dollar business deal.

2. Listen to your teen actively without talking over them or thinking of how you will respond to what they are saying.

3. Help your teen communicate their feelings by teaching them feeling words they can use to express themselves.

4. Loosen the grip on control and only maintain as much control as necessary. Give your teen choices and help them make the right decisions using curious questions.

5. As a positive parenting principle, tell you, children, as often as possible that mistakes are a

wonderful opportunity to learn and demonstrate recognition, responsibility, reconciliation, and resolution.

Chapter Five

Enabling vs. Empowering

Sometimes, it feels good when people do things for us that we could do for ourselves. However, when parents do this for their teens, it's called enabling. Enabling is doing for teens the things we know they can do for themselves. Enabling usually comes from fear and lack of trust that the teens can't handle themselves.

Empowering, on the other hands, is being in the middle of your teen's life but by standing on the sideline to support and encourage them. Let's take a soccer match, for instance. Your daughter just joined the soccer team and will be playing her match this Saturday. Naturally, she has asked you to drive her to the game, and you have accepted. When you get to the field, would you change into her uniform and replace her in the team because you are afraid that she might make a mistake and cost the team a win?

Not! Like other parents, you will find a seat on the side and cheer her from there. Your daughter, on the other hand, knows the responsibility she holds by playing a forward in the team. She knows her team is depending on her to make the right judgment and score when an opportunity opens up. She knows that she needs to work with her team to open up opportunities and score.

As if that is not enough, she is aware of all the soccer rules she needs to follow lest she earns herself a red card and is disqualified from the game. Without a doubt, as she plays, she observes as many rules as possible although she makes a mistake or two. When the game is over, the coach calls the team together, and they discuss the outcome. Whether they won or not, they look at the mistakes they made and how they can be improved in the coming games.

It's the same with rearing teens. To empower them to be their best and become the best versions of themselves, we have to learn to stay on the side and watch them play the game of life. They are bound to make mistakes every once in a while, sometimes more than we would like them to, but our job is just to gather them and empower them to make better decisions in the future.

If we rescue them or try to control them, we are not preparing them for life in the right way. Some of the typical enabling behavior we get into include fixing their lunch, picking out their clothes, and doing their laundry limits their exposure to learning. Sometimes, parents type out papers for their teens, deliver forgotten homework, or to school are also enabling their teens.

If your teen skips school and you lie to their teacher, you are enabling them. Excusing teens from helping around the house because they have much homework is also enabling them. If you pretend that everything is ok because you want to avoid a confrontation, you are enabling your teen.

Positive parenting is based on empowerment principles. This includes teaching and giving emotional support without rescuing your teen, teaching life skills, letting go without abandoning your teen, sharing your thoughts, and feelings without lecturing, arguing, or controlling, and working on agreements.

It is normal for you as a parent to feel that like you are doing nothing when you first start practicing these principles. You are used to punishing, controlling, or rescuing, which makes positive parenting uncomfortable. That's perfectly ok. At first, your teen may even resist and insist that you go back to being the drill sergeant because they already know what to expect. They will make you feel guilty because you did not rush to rescue them when they called you, but don't give in to the temptation. Short-term solutions will produce half-baked individuals.

Let us compare some enabling and empowering statements you could practice.

Enabling: I can't believe you procrastinated again. What will you become if you don't finish your homework? I'll do your laundry this once, so you have time to finish your homework.

Empowering: What is your picture regarding what is going on with your homework? Would like to brainstorm ideas on how you can get everything done on time?

Enabling: Sweetie I thought when I bought you a car, a cellphone and increased your allowance, you would finish your chores on time and do your homework.

Empowering: I know you are upset about getting that poor grade. It's a bummer. I have faith in you, and I know you can figure out how to balance your chores and school work.

Enabling: I will increase our allowance if you do your homework on time. I will even buy you a cellphone.

Empowering: I'm sorry, but I'm not willing to bail you out. When your teacher calls, I will hand the phone to you so that you can discuss it with her.

Enabling: Ok, I will write a note to your teacher this once so you can stay at home. But you must promise to catch up.

Empowering: I'm happy to talk about college options with you, but I am not sure if it's important to you.

How to Teach your Teens Life Skills
Look for Teachable Moments

Kids, including teens, learn quickly, but parents tend to underutilize their ability to learn. Teens don't learn by being told what to do but by being involved and when parents engage with them. You will get many opportunities to teach life skills such as money, clothing, sex, and family work. For instance, Tom had early class on Friday, and it took mountains to get him out of bed on time for class. He would constantly argue with his father Da about it as he woke him up, telling him to get off his back.

Dan received a letter from Tom's teacher saying that if he missed one more time, he would fail the class. Dan waited till Thursday to talk to Tom about it. He picked up Tom from school that day, but instead of lecturing him about the letter and the fact that he was about to fail, he took a different turn.

"I received a letter from your teacher today. She said that if you miss one more time, you will fail the class. Do you want to go to class tomorrow or do you want to miss and fail?

"I guess I'll have to go."

"Do you want me to wake you up or will you wake up by yourself?"

"I will wake myself up."

"All right, I will leave you alone." And that's exactly what Dan did. Tom woke up on time and made it to class for the rest of the term.

Use your Teen's Interests to Teach

Some of the best teaching moments can be found when you use your teen's interests to teach life skills. Teen girls are preoccupied with clothing and shopping, which is a perfect time to teach your daughter about money, budgeting, and planning. You can use your son's interest in cars to be a great moment to teach about saving, discipline, and obedience on the road and in life.

Pauline always warned her daughter Betty about loaning her expensive clothes, but she never listened. They argued about it, and Pauline realized she was handling the situation all wrong. Talking was going to get her nowhere. She apologized for trying to 'ruin' her daughters' friendships and promised not to interfere again. She never did.

One evening, her daughter came home in a rage. One of her best friends has lost her designer bag at a party. Pauline fought as hard as possible to hide her smile, and instead of starting with the "I told you so" lecture, she empathized with her and gave her a big hug. "I can see how upset you are; I am so sorry."

"I'll never let her borrow my stuff again."

"Would you like me to give you an idea of loaning clothes?"

"Sure."

"You can tell your friend you want a deposit or one of their nice stuff to hold on to until they return yours. This is called collateral."

"Thanks, but I don't think that would work with my friends. They have no idea what it's like to be on a clothing allowance because they get anything they want. I won't let them borrow my stuff."

"Good plan. "

Teach your Teens how to Plan

Life is full of busy schedules, and teens need to learn how to schedule and plan well in advance. Making all plans by yourself is easier but denies your teen the opportunity to learn how to plan and create schedules. Your teen will also not have an idea of what is planned, and they will expect you to do everything for them and rescue them when things go wrong.

Although it takes more time, involving your teen in the schedule will show respect and teach them life skills. Planning a family meeting to discuss upcoming events and make a schedule that works for everyone is a great idea. Many parents complain that they don't have time, but they don't factor in the time spent doing chores they should not be doing and the frustration involved in those instances.

This can be avoided when everyone is involved in what is happening, and when they know the role, they need to play to make things work. Olivia was about to open school. For a long time, her mother was a stay at home mom for a while, and she could manage to drop her and pick her from school. However, she had just gotten a job she was excited about and would not be available to take her anymore.

Two weeks before school opened, she asked her mom if they could make a schedule around her work. Once they had established how many days her mom would be available to drop her and pick her, Olivia organized to carpool with her friends the other days. She also needed some school supplies bought before schools opened, so they planned which day would be best to go shopping for school supplies and school clothes.

Keith was in a situation of his own parents. He wanted to attend a concert by his favorite musician, but it was fifty miles away. He had no driving licenses or a car and would need one of his parents to take him. Every time he asked them to talk about it and come up with a solution, his parents said they were busy and postponed the meeting. Because they didn't get back to him in time, so he missed the concert. His parents had no idea they were rude and disrespectful. They thought his plans were not important, so they kept putting him off until he missed the convert.

This is not an unusual occurrence. Jasmine wanted to go to a dance, but her parents were not comfortable with the fact her she would be in the company of a boy all evening. They kept postponing the decision until it was too late for Jasmine to go to the dance. Jasmine was denied the opportunity to make arrangements with her plan on where they would eat, the dresses they would wear and what time they would be back home. Keith, on the other hand, could not make arrangements with his friends to attend the concert or to carpool with any of his friends. Both Keith and Jasmine will enter adulthood with limited planning and scheduling skills.

Teach your teen to get over their fear as you get over yours

Many teens prefer that their parents make decisions for them and control them because they are afraid of growing up. As a parent, if you feed this fear with your own, your teen won't develop the skill they need to become successful adults. The best way to help your teen build courage is to them your enthusiasm for their growing process.

"Won't it be exciting when you grow up and leave home for college?"

"Aren't you looking forward to your first full-time job?"

"Are you excited about your picking your first apartment?"

Your excitement will be contagious and will help your teen look forward to growing up. The most important thing is teaching them step-by-step by encouraging them before you leave them on their own to exercise what they have learned.

Let's assume Jasmine was allowed to go to the dance. At the mall, she would have used her clothing allowance to find a pretty dress and possibly shop for a bargain to get something that looks incredible at a lower price. Also, she would have made plans on how much she planned to spend on food, makeup, and accessories for the night. If the money she had were not enough, she would have learned how to stretch it to fit her budget or what to forego to get the items she wanted.

All these are skills she would need as an adult. When she gets a job, she may be tempted to spend all her money on clothes, but because she learned some money skills during her teen years, she will budget for rent, food, cellphone, gas, savings, clothes and everything else she needs before her next paycheck. When things are tight, she will cook at home instead of eating at a restaurant and skip going to the bar until she can afford drinks. All these are skills Jasmine will have cultivated during adolescence.

Encourage Routines

The practice is the only way to become better at something. While bad routines are easy to fall into, good routines need a little more thought and planning. Instead of nagging your slightly overweight daughter about losing weight, Kelly told her she wanted to learn how to dance but was not sure how to bust the moves. She had signed up for a class and wanted to find out if her Annie would be interested in joining because she loved dancing, Annie was interested and even offered to show Kelly a few moves before the class, so she wasn't so green.

A few weeks later, Kelly has improved on her dancing, and Annie had not only become a better dancer than she was, but she had also trimmed down considerably. The two continued to dance together and even won a competition at Annie's school. Repetition makes the routine so don't be afraid to ask your teen to commit to several classes before you commit your money and time to drive them around.

Don't be Afraid to ask for Help

Sometimes, teens don't listen to us because we are their parents, but they are willing to listen to other adults they hold in high regard. For example, if your teen is on the soccer team, you probably don't have as much impact on them as the coach does, especially if they think the coach is the best thing that has ever happened to his team.

Also, a teen is likely to listen to a tutor more when homework is concerned than she is likely to listen to you. If the tutor tells you to stop nagging your teen, you will listen and back off to give your teen some space. The same thing applies to your teen. If the tutor suggests homework, they are likely to listen and follow through than when the suggestion is coming from you.

There is nothing wrong with asking your teen's coach, tutor, dance class teacher, or the school lecture to collaborate with you to teach a life skill. If you can't get through to your teen, there must be an adult who can. Find them and ask them to help you out. Most people will be glad to help you because we all want the same thing for teens: to rear independent, responsible adults.

Make sure that your teen does not find out that you are asking others for help. Teens hate to be discussed, and this will blow up in your face if you don't warn your helper.

Also, kids who are interested in non-academic activities create more opportunities to interact with people who will have a positive impact on their lives. As a parent, encourage your teen to sign up for a class and invest the money necessary for them to pursue the class, trip, or competition.

Chapter Six

What to do About Scary Behavior

Certain topics are at the top of every teen parent's agenda because they are scary not just to us, but also to our teens. These include friends, or lack thereof, drug and alcohol abuse, sexual activity, abuse and diseases, suicidal behaviors, eating disorders or problems, and young adults who refuse to leave home. In this chapter, we will show you how to use positive parenting principles to handle these scary behaviors and set your teen up for success and independence. Let's dive in.

Friends or Lack Thereof

Friends are vital to a teen's development and growth, so when your teen separates themselves from peers for longer than necessary, it raises a red flag for you as a parent. For teens who are willing to listen to suggestions, you can suggest that your teen starts by changing his/her mental attitude. If they feel insecure, they will act insecure. A teen who feels confident acts confident, and since confidence is attractive, they are likely to attract friends.

Ask your teen to practice smiling when walking through the school halls. She should also be genuinely interested in other people and be curious about them. You can encourage your teen to get involved in activities that will put in position them to interact with others. They can join the school band if they are interested in music, the debate cloud, science club or a sport. Also, insist that your teen try something at least four times before they quit.

Teens need to understand that rejection is part of life, and just because a few people have rejected them does not mean they are bad, undeserving, unattractive, or they don't have pleasing personalities. Encourage them to take risks to ask a group if they can join in. They may get rejected 80% of the time, but 20% will accept them. The teen's focus should be on the 20% who accepted, not the 80% who declined.

What if you Hate your Teen's Friends?

Many battles are fought because parents don't like friends their teens choose. This is reasonable considering the number of influence friends has on teens. However, parents handle this in a way that pushes teens to be loyal to the very friends their parents don't like. Very few, if any, parents have been able to forbid their teens from seeing certain friends successfully.

Instead of trying to control your teen, invite their friends over to your home and try to get to know them better. You will either be surprised that they are not as bad as you thought, or your teen will grow tired of them by themselves. Teens can't keep bad company for long, and even naughty teens find a balance with time and leave their wayward ways with the right guidance.

Be honest about your fears with your teen and use the positive principle in this book to equip them with skills they can use to deal with the potentially dangerous situation if it ever occurs.

Drugs and Alcohol Abuse

This is one of the scariest behavior parents have to face. You know the probability of someone sneaking a pill into your teen's drinks at a party that would end up in rape or worse. You also know the experiments teens get into by crushing pills in their parent's medicine cabinets and drowning them to see what happens.

Parents fear drugs and alcohol because they used to abuse them when they were teens. Other parents may have never abused drugs, but they have fears because they are not sure if their teens will abstain as well. Some parents are not even aware it's a problem until they catch their teen using. There is much denials that accompanies drug use, and most parents would rather take their teens for mental illness diagnosis than admit they are using drugs.

But what makes drugs so popular among teens even with the detrimental health complications they cause and the scare they give parents? Teens say they want to experiment and find out the effect the drug has; others use them to belong to a group, while others feel it takes away their shyness, makes them fun, sexier, relaxed and free. For teens who have a rough time, drugs are a way to numb their feelings. So how do you deal with this scary behavior?

Some teens will listen when you tell them that you don't want them to use drugs, so this is the first step you should take. Also, some teens use drugs when they are idle, so enrolling them in activities that will keep them preoccupied is a good plan. This may not entirely tackle the problem, but all efforts are required to get your teen sober.

Although your teen may not engage in drugs and alcohol abuse, make sure you educate them on the effects of drugs, and addiction to substances has on them and the people around them. Caution them to look out for signs such as vomiting, mental confusion, seizures, slow breathing, and passing out. If it happens to a friend, they should call for help immediately.

The best way to help them make informed decisions is to empower them in every aspect using the principles taught in this book. When teens feel listened to, understood, and taken seriously, and know they can talk to you anytime and about anything, they are less likely to get involved with drugs. The reality is, your teen may choose to use drugs whether you stay vigilant or not, whether you like it or not.

However, there are differences in drug use. There is abstinence which is staying away from drugs altogether and experimental use, which means your teen heard about it and wants to try to see how it feels like. A teen may try a drug once and never again if they are just experimenting. This does not make drug use any less scary, but if you find out, do not overreact.

Social use, on the other hand, means your teen used drugs during social occasions, but he or she does not let the drugs take over. A social user can easily stop after a certain amount while an addict will continue to use. Social use may still be a concern because, with practice, people get better. Tell your teen what you think, how you feel, and what you expect from them and be as clear as possible. You should then ask your teen what they think, feel, and want, and practice the listening skills you talked about in the earlier chapter.

A regular drug user has ritualized drug use, which makes it potentially more dangerous to your teen because it could easily turn into an addiction. Some teens may be able to maintain their school life, relationships, and self-respect while smoking every day, but the likelihood of this becoming a serious problem is high.

Problem use happens when teens are unable to function normally in society because of drugs. The more teens use drugs, the less they develop their skills. If you think their use is problematic, tell them you love them and that you want to help them help. Don't accept promises to change. Your teen may be sincere in their desire to change, but they have no idea the hold the drug has on them. You should not expect your teen to reason with you. Instead, you should seek help as soon as possible to avoid the next stage.

Chemical dependency occurs when the drug takes over and runs your teen's life. Drug use starts as a harmless activity, but it can grow to a monster that takes over.

Understanding the stages of drug use and helping your teen understand them as well puts you at a better position to handle it in the event it occurs. There is a lot of help available for parents struggling with teenagers abusing drugs. Get all the support you need by engaging friends, relatives, and therapists.

Teen Sex, Pregnancy and Sexually Transmitted Diseases

Most parents want to think that their teens are abstinent, waiting until they give them the big talk, but in most cases, that is not how the script plays out. Teenage sex is increasing, and studies show that a high number of boys and girl are active by the age of seventeen and some as early as junior high.

Prohibiting sex does not guarantee that your teens will not be sexually active, and neither does raising your kids believing in religious laws governing sex. Sex is addictive, and dropping your daughter off in the morning and picking her up after school does not guarantee abstinence.

Positive parenting advocates for keeping open lines of communication between our teens and us. As parents, we need to openly express our beliefs and moral values on the topic in a clear, sensitive, and straightforward way. We should also include what health specialists are telling us about the physical, mental, emotional, and sexuality effects teen sex have on our teens.

Raising kids who openly share with us their hopes, aspirations, dreams, and sexuality puts us in pretty good shape to help them answer the questions they have regarding sex and other issues. Teens will often ask parents about their sexuality, which is common where sexual matters are openly discussed. The best advice we can give them is to answer as generally as possible and to keep all specifics to yourself. This reserves your right to privacy while helping your teen understand sex.

Most parents don't know what to answer when their kids ask why they should not have sex. If you find yourself in this situation, tell your teen that you would like them to enjoy sex for the rest of their lives, but if they engage now and end up feeling shameful, bad or guilty, it will affect the joy of enjoying sex later. Besides that, there are sexually transmitted diseases such as AIDS to think about. That is why you would want them to wait until they meet someone they feel good about.

But, if they choose to go with a different choice, you hope they will come to you first so that you can see a physician about contraception and just talk it over with them first.

Telling your teen just to say no will not work with sexually, the same way it does not work with drugs and alcohol. By telling them you are willing to talk things out with them does not give them the green light to engage in sex either, but at least it gives them time to think their decision over, protect themselves and be sure that they are making the right choice for them.

Teens should also be given facts about STDs, AIDS, and the risk of pregnancy by talking about them in a cool, loving, and matter of fact manner. By openly communicating with your teen about sex, you are sending them the message that you trust them and believe they are old enough to make the right choice.

Suicidal Behavior

Sadly, suicide is one of the leading causes of death among teens. It is a scary behavior that parents must take everything seriously when recognizing if the suicidal threats are manipulative in nature or something to be taken seriously. If your teen has indirectly mentioned suicide, or you have reason to be concerned, it is wise that you talk about it as the thought has already crossed your teen's mind.

Talk to your teen about it, show them that you care while matter-of-factly stating the facts. Refrain from telling your teen what to feel by telling them "you don't mean that" or "don't ever talk like that again" as it only makes matters worse. If depression or suicide runs in the family, the risk could be higher, so be cautious.

Teens who are most at risk are those who achieve without struggle, and those who try and never seem to succeed. On the one hand, one teen expects success to be automatic, so when it is not, they cannot handle it. On the other hand, one teen feels hopeless that no matter how hard they try, things keep falling apart.

As a parent, your goal as you discuss suicide should be to help your teen pursue other option to express themselves. You should also consider other avenues such as support groups, counseling and if necessary, hospitalization. Explore alternatives with your child without forcing them to decide on the spot. Be loving, calm, and receptive without downplaying the problem. If the threats escalate or lead to an actual attempt, seek professional help.

Kids who Won't Move Out

Most children who live at home stay because they grew accustomed to a certain lifestyle that their parents helped them to become accustomed to, and now they are afraid they can't afford the lifestyle by themselves. Others stay home because their rescue parents have convinced them they can't make it on their own and they need them to hover over their every decision. In some rare occasions, some kids have not found jobs after college, and they can't afford to rent a place of their own.

The bottom line is, if your teen stays home for a free ride and does not help you with anything, that's a problem. If they are actively looking for work and helping you around the house, this could be a temporary problem for them. Even when jobs are hard to come by, teens can live with friends sharing rent, rooms, and couches.

The best thing you can do for adult kids who are still living at home is to move them out eventually. Give them a deadline and expect them to meet it. Offer to help them get a job and drive them to an interview if need be.

Sometimes, older kids may need to move back home to get a fresh start, but this should not be used as a way to bail them out of the financial crisis they willingly brought upon themselves. If an older kid needs to move back home, ask them what's in it for you. Remember, you will now play the role of a parent and a landlord. If it isn't a win-win situation, it will be a lose-lose situation, and you should not agree to it. They should also not spend the time hanging out, but they should actively be seeking ways to be out of their financial situation, regain stability, and find their place again.

Conclusion

Parenting teens comes with its fair share of challenges, but if you employ positive parenting principles, the ride will be fun and relaxed. Teens go through tons of changes during these short years, and their brains and bodies change to that of an adult. You should learn to loosen your grip on control and treat them in a way that shows concern, care, and trust while letting them own their problems and face the consequences of their actions.

Positive parenting does not mean that teens will behave like a mini-adult and avoid the many troublesome behaviors that come with this time of their lives, but it helps to equip parent on dealing with this behavior, using mistakes a learning tool and teaching teens life skills that they can take with them into adulthood.

Every parent is delighted to see their child happy and successful, and we cannot achieve this if we become fearful parents that try to control everything our teens do or hover over them like helicopters when there is no real emergency. By being thoughtful, loving consultants, we can achieve much more and empower our teens to be responsible, reasonable adults who are capable of forming meaningful relationships, standing on their values and believing in who they are no matter the challenges they face.

References

Bluestein, Jane, Ph.D. and Lynn Collins, M.A, Parents In A Pressure Cooker. Modern Learning Press, 1989.

Johnson, Kendall, Ph.D., Turning Yourself Around: Self-Help Strategies For Troubled Teens. Hunter House, 1992.

Bluestein, Jane, Ph.D., Parenting Teens, And Boundaries. Health Communications, Inc, 1993.

Nelson, Jane, ED.D, Lynn Lott, M.A, Positive Discipline For Teens. Harmony Books, 2012

Foster Cline, Jim Fay, Parenting Teens with Love and Logic. Navpress, 2014

Brookshire Bethany, Hormone Affects How Teens Brain Control Emotions. ScienceNews for Students, Jul 15, 2016

Tyborowska Ann et al., Testosterone During Puberty Shifts Emotional Control from Pulvinar To Anterior Prefrontal Cortex. JNeurosci, June 8, 2016.

47680718R00152

Printed in Poland
by Amazon Fulfillment
Poland Sp. z o.o., Wrocław